# Service

# in a

# Sari

The Story of Nan Dunlop
Missionary in Central India

**ERNEST C BROWN**

**EVANGELICAL PRESBYTERIAN CHURCH**

15 College Square East BELFAST BT1 6QD

© Evangelical Presbyterian Church 1996
*First Published 1996*

ISBN 0 9522662 1 0

Cover Picture
*An Outing near Chhapara*
Courtesy - Dr Helen Ramsay

Children - Top to bottom and left to right:
Arun, Sharan, Santosh, Vijai, Vinai

Cover Design:  Vincent McDonnell

Distributors:
Evangelical Book Shop
15 College Square East
BELFAST BT1 6QD

Telephone  01232 320529

Printed by J C Print Ltd Belfast

# Contents

# Dedication

To the memory of Nan's mother, Isabella Dunlop.

Without her Christian influence, her love, and her evangelistic zeal for the world, Nan may never have been a missionary.

# Foreword

My service in India overlapped with Nan Dunlop's for a mere few weeks. But in that short time I came to love and respect her. Her devotion to the Lord, adaptation to the Indian ways and language, enthusiasm for evangelism and burden for the Indian people were a great stimulus to a new missionary.

Two small incidents among others, illustrating Nan's sanctified common sense and feeling for people, remain in my mind. Discussing the daunting prospect of language study and adaptation to life in a rather underdeveloped hospital where I would be expected to set up a surgical service, I voiced my fear of making mistakes. Nan immediately replied, "The man who never made a mistake never made anything!" No doubt I made my share of mistakes, but, by God's grace and with the help of many colleagues, I was enabled to build something worthwhile on the labours of former missionaries.

One early Sunday, on the way down to church in Lakhnadon village my 2½ year old son, Colin, whom I was carrying on my shoulders, accidentally knocked off my dark glasses and one of the legs broke. I showed my annoyance with a sharp rebuke. But Nan immediately interceded for Colin, pointing out that he didn't mean to do it. Nan always showed that understanding for people, especially the weak and defenceless. I had to learn to curb my natural impatience!

Nan left India at a time of transition for our mission. The medical work became part of the Emmanuel Hospital Association, the hospital base was strengthened, more Indian staff recruited and community health village outreach programmes instituted. I believe Nan would have adapted to the new pattern of working and would have brought her own inimitable style of evangelism to bear on the many new opportunities that were afforded. However, it was not to be, and we had to say goodbye to her before we could benefit most from her help. But her example was always before us.

It is my prayer that this warm-hearted, yet realistic account of one humble Christian's missionary service will challenge you afresh to whole-hearted commitment to serving Christ wherever you are called to do so.

"God chose the foolish things of the world to shame the wise; God chose the weak things of the world to shame the strong." (1 Corinthians 1:27)

D M MacDonald FRCSEd

# Introduction

At a congregational outing of Stranmillis Evangelical Presbyterian Church to Bangor, Co Down, on an evening in May 1994, I attached myself to Nan Dunlop and began to talk to her as we walked along the promenade. I had planned this little chat and I had planned the topic of conversation too - a book about her life as a missionary with the Free Church of Scotland in Central India. I was not the originator of this idea. Credit for that belongs to Dr Anne Urquhart, missionary colleague of Nan's for twelve years, and author of *Near India's Heart*, the official history of the Free Church's missionary work in India. She had suggested the project to Nan some years before and Nan had mentioned it to me, not at all as a hint to put it into effect, but purely in appreciation of Dr Urquhart's generosity in proposing it. We did not 'sign a contract' that evening in Bangor, for Nan was very hesitant about adopting such a profile. But as she reflected a little on the purposes - to give thanks to God for her life's work, and to quicken missionary interest in the church - she became persuaded.

How the book came together is a story for another time, but here I wish to thank a number of contributors: Nan's former missionary colleagues provided a wealth of reminiscences—informative, humorous and generous. Rev Prakash Kumar, minister of the Chhapara congregation of the Free Church of Central India and Mr Alexander John, Headmaster of Chhapara Christian School who grew up in the mission orphanage and knew Nan well from their childhood, wrote appreciatively. And it was a pleasure to include some recollections from Mrs Sarah MacLeod, widow of Rev Murray MacLeod, Superintendent of the mission when Nan arrived in 1944.

Mrs Macleod lives in Ontario, Canada, and is now in her 88th year.

Several very busy friends and partners in missionary interest read the manuscript for me, and made very valuable suggestions: Rev Dr Donald MacDonald, whom I also thank for writing the Foreword, Dr Anne Urquhart, Principal A C Boyd, Rev Gareth Burke, Rev Derek Thomas, and John Grier. Julia Grier did the proof-reading.

I include in the acknowledgements the Presbytery of the Evangelical Presbyterian Church for publishing the book, the Evangelical Book Shop, for distributing, Vincent McDonnell for designing the cover, and Rev Gavin Smith for the title.

I also wish to thank Knox Press, Edinburgh, for permission to quote from *Near India's Heart*. It has been my constant companion throughout the project and I have depended upon it for background and reference. I have been anxious to avoid duplication with it, except in so far as this has been necessary in presenting Nan's life in the context of the developing mission story. I commend it warmly to our readers.

Most of all I wish to thank Nan Dunlop herself for her patience and diligence in helping me write this account. In addition to providing much of the material for the book, she has discussed my endless questions, and given many hours to reading progressive manuscript drafts. I count it one of my greatest privileges to have worked with her, to have listened to her vivid memories, and to have absorbed something more of her wonderful missionary spirit. It is Nan's wish that any proceeds from the sale of the book are used for the continuing work in India.

*Ernest C Brown*  Belfast, April 1996

# Only a Sinner

Naught have I gotten but what I received;
Grace hath bestowed it and I have believed;
Boasting excluded, pride I abase;
I'm only a sinner saved by grace!

*Only a sinner saved by grace!*
*Only a sinner saved by grace!*
*This is my story, to God be the glory, -*
*I'm only a sinner saved by grace!*

Once I was foolish, and sin ruled my heart,
Causing my footsteps from God to depart;
Jesus hath found me, happy my case;
I now am a sinner, saved by grace!

Tears unavailing, no merit had I;
Mercy had saved me, or else I must die;
Sin had alarmed me, fearing God's face;
But now I'm a sinner, saved by grace!

Suffer a sinner whose heart overflows,
Loving his Saviour to tell what he knows;
Once more to tell it would I embrace -
I'm only a sinner, saved by grace!

*James M Gray 1851-1935*

# 1

# Dear Mother...

Mission House
Lakhnadon
Dist Seoni
M.P.
India
1 Aug 1959

My Dear Mam

It's awful I haven't written since I came back from the hills. I can hardly credit it. I'm well now and as the rain is on it's cooler. It was awfully hot when I got back and I took both babies for a while until Helen got the other children off to school. Now I have Vimala. She is a dear wee thing and Tarabai is a big help with her. I have no worry when I go out to a patient at all, as I know that the baby will be well looked after.

We get a lot of in-patients here and a lot of calls out. I was out to one maternity case where we went out 25 miles by road and then ten miles out on horseback with the rain raining on us. We went out and back in one day. There were no stirrups, so the man tied two pieces of cloth for me to put my feet in but I was sore with sitting on the horse. On the way back as we crossed a stream we heard a tiger roar in the distance and the horse didn't like it. That was on a Sunday. On another Sunday I had been 25 miles out to a service and 25 back. Then I had a visit to make in Lakhnadon and at 10.00 pm a call came for a maternity case right out the same 25 miles. This time I went in a lorry. The doctor and nurse had been with the patient all day and she was in a critical condition. I got the doctor persuaded after two hours to give the patient an anaesthetic and we had the baby there in about ten minutes. The baby's arm had been showing since 2.00 pm in the afternoon and it wasn't born until 2.00 am. I got home at 5.00 am and before I had finished the morning dispensary there was another call twelve miles out in a bus and a four or five mile walk. I was there all night too so I was quite tired when I got back.

I have had quite a lot of calls. There was one woman I couldn't deliver so we brought her back through the jungle in the night on a bed and then I took her to Seoni. The civil surgeon delivered her but she died two hours after. The next one who needed Caesarian we took to Nagpur. Helen is busy with out-patients, but I seem to be busy with in-patients and calls. I had an in-patient last week-end who was very ill and semi-conscious but she came round and was doing nicely. Then the first night everyone went to sleep she died of heart failure. I was a bit upset but what could one do.

The people at Ghansore have asked for a Sunday service. That is 25 miles away but I try to go. I didn't go last week because of floods and the ill patient. I haven't been able to say half of what I wanted to say. Must stop. Will write soon.

Love and blessings

Nan

PS There aren't many months left until I get home and sometimes I can hardly wait. Love Nan.

# 2

# The Making of a Missionary

## At Home

Annie Johnstone Dunlop, the eldest of her family, was born on 17th May 1918, when World War I was entering its final six months. She was born in Havelock Place in the lower Ormeau Road district of south Belfast, which lies midway between the River Lagan and Belfast city centre, and about ten minutes walk from each. On the opposite side of the Ormeau Road was Belfast Gasworks whose size and storage tanks dominated the locality at that time, and where much of the local employment was provided. Nan's first address was 'Havelock Cottage', a dwelling detached from the rows of terraced houses, which lined the cobbled streets. Later, when the family moved a stone's throw away to a house in Outram Street, the cottage was re-developed and became 'Havelock Street Belfast City Mission.' Later generations will know the location from its modern landmark—the studios of Ulster Television. Nan was born just behind them.

Nan's mother, Annabella Gilmour (usually known as Isabella), came from Bangor in County Down and her family belonged to the local Presbyterian Church at Ballygilbert. Both Isabella's parents died in her early childhood, her father as a result of a drowning accident, and consequently, when she was about six, she went to live with her maternal grandparents in Killyleagh, a village in the same county, and grew up there. Like many girls in her generation, she found employment in going into service, in her case with a family at Craigantlet, a locality between Belfast and Bangor, not far from her childhood home. It is not known how she met her husband Hugh Dunlop, who was from Belfast, but it appears that his family had connections in the Killyleagh area where he was a regular visitor before the Great War. Appropriately, Isabella and Hugh were married in Ballygilbert Presbyterian Church.

Mrs Dunlop was converted in 1922 at one of the W P Nicholson evangelistic campaigns and became a very bright, active, and witnessing Christian. She was a powerful influence both in the home and outside it. She brought the children up to have family worship; she read and explained the Bible to them; she taught them the need for salvation; she made them familiar with Christian books. She made sure they went to church, and if not there herself, for she had a series of health problems, she always had to know who was preaching and the content of the sermon. And they had to remember. Outside the home, Mrs Dunlop was always trying to get unconverted people to Gospel meetings, and she helped with arranging something for them to wear if that was needed. Someone who used to visit her in the late 1960's, when she was 80 or a little more, has paid this tribute which so aptly sums her up: "She was a tremendous character who naturally and delightfully dominated the room."

Nan's father Hugh had fought in the First Word War. He took part in the Battle of the Somme in northern France in 1916 where he sustained injuries which not only ended his own participation in the war, but left their mark on him for the rest of his life. The trench from which he was fighting collapsed and he lay buried in it for three days while the battle raged above him. He was brought home to hospital in St Stephen's Green in Dublin and spent six months there before being transferred to a military hospital at Galwally in Belfast. He married Isabella after his recovery. However the effect of his injuries was prolonged and he continued to receive treatment at Galwally periodically in later years. As an index of the severity of his injuries, he was awarded an 80% war disability pension. Interestingly, his War Office citation described him as 'buried in France.'

By trade he was a Hydraulic Crane Operator, working in the nearby Belfast Gasworks unloading coal from the barges or 'lighters' as they were called, which brought supplies along the Lagan and Blackstaff Rivers to the Gasworks. He was not comfortable with the idea of electric cranes, and when they began to displace their hydraulic predecessors, he moved to other duties. He had an interesting pastime too—a donkey which he trained to provide entertainment with some simple routines.

Hugh was converted a few years after his wife, whose influence played an important part. He had a different personality and temperament from hers. He was less out-going than she was, but was firm, and exerted a very steadying influence. He never lost his temper. Whereas Nan's mother would have administered summary justice, her father's approach could be more instructive. Nan remembers an example of his reproof: "Now you're much older than she is and you should have more sense." He used to sing hymns in the house and he sang with the children. He would join in discussion with visitors about the spiritual topics of the day such as the W P Nicholson evangelistic campaign.

Before we leave the family scene we should explain the background to the name 'Nan.' As a child Annie did not like her name. Her mother offered to call her 'John' as an abbreviation of 'Johnstone', her middle name, but she didn't like that either. However she was quite happy with 'Nan' or 'Nancy' and her mother often called her one of these. The contemporary song, 'Nancy Gray of the hearts of Down', provided an enjoyable comparison within the family. Outside the home she continued to be known as Annie by most people during her pre-missionary years. Later when she began to work with Dr Annie Mackay in India, 'Nan' was the ready-made solution and before long it became the familiar name.

## At School

Nan started going to the local church's nursery school for a few hours a day when she was only three. She remembers her first nursery teacher, Miss Bell, as a lovely person. When she was six she moved to Primary School. The school leaving age then was fourteen, and although Nan had finished the work by the time she was twelve, she had to mark time until she could take the Higher Grade Certificate at the specified leaving age. Nan has every reason not to forget her first Primary teacher either— Miss Boyd, who stayed with the class as they progressed through grades 1-4. Miss Boyd on occasions 'hammered' her and sometimes sent her to the Headmaster. What for? "For talking and bad spelling." But Nan was sure that Miss Boyd liked her all the same, and she had confirmation of this after she left school, when Miss Boyd invited her to her own home on the Malone Road. She talked to Nan again about her spelling, reminding her of 'i before e except after c', and so on, and as Nan was leaving she gave her a little gift—a book about spelling.

## At Church

Mrs Dunlop sent Nan to two Sunday Schools from the age of three—to a morning Sunday School in the local city church the family attended, and to another in the neighbourhood in the afternoon. She had a sharp conflict of opinion with the minister about Nan going to this other Sunday School. But this was not the only problem. Mrs Dunlop was already concerned that the family were learning very little at the church and was beginning to look elsewhere. Doubtless the minister's hostile, disparaging attitude towards the other Sunday School did nothing to change her mind.

The Irish Evangelical Church, which became Nan's church from the time she was nine, was formed in 1927 as a result of the Heresy Trial in the Irish Presbyterian Church that year. Among the issues at stake were the Inerrancy of Scripture, the Deity of Christ, and the need for a sincere subscription to the Confession of Faith. The early story was told in *The Origin and Witness of the Irish Evangelical Church*, 1945, by Rev W J Grier. Rev G N M Collins of Edinburgh said in the Foreword: "I regard it not only as a token of personal friendship on the part of the author of this interesting little book that he should ask me to write this Foreword, but also, and especially, as a mark of the friendship of the Irish Evangelical Church, whose story he tells in these pages, for the Free Church of Scotland in which it is my privilege to minister. And in token of reciprocal regard, both personal and denominational, I have the utmost pleasure in complying with his request. For the witness of the Irish Evangelical Church, and that

*c. 1920*

*SRN, SCM, 1942*

*1955*

*1965*

of the Free Church of Scotland, if not identical, are so similar that the most cordial relations have always existed between the two bodies." The church changed its name in 1964 to *Evangelical Presbyterian Church* to reflect more clearly its Presbyterian history and convictions, and to identify it more closely with its subordinate standards—the Westminster Confession of Faith and Catechisms. A new history of the denomination is expected in October 1997 to mark its 70th anniversary.

Hugh Dunlop was well disposed towards the new, emerging church. Before 'Shaftesbury Square', its first congregation, moved to Botanic Avenue in August 1930, he walked two miles with the family to the Lisburn Road church which opened in April 1928. But it was too far for the children to walk back for Sunday School in the afternoon. Rev W J Grier was the Lisburn Road minister at that time and he baptised Nan's youngest brother Lawrence, who was the first child to be baptised in the Irish Evangelical Church. Hugh Dunlop joined Botanic Avenue in 1931, and Mrs Isabella Dunlop in 1932. The membership book shows that by then they had moved to Fernwood Street, further up the Ormeau Road, and further from Lisburn Road. Mrs Dunlop loved the country, and the open space around Fernwood Street at that time was one of the factors which made the move attractive. Nan was a first generation pupil in Botanic Avenue Sunday School and became a church member in June 1936.

It was in Fernwood Street that Nan formed a lasting friendship with Margaret Williamson, who later married Frederick S Leahy, well known as a minister of the Reformed Presbyterian Church of Ireland, and Professor of Systematic Theology at the church's Reformed Theological College, before becoming Principal. The Williamsons had lived for a time in Canada where Margaret was born, and when they returned to Northern Ireland they went back to their previous locality of Ballynahinch. Mr Williamson found work in Inglis Bakery in Belfast but this required a round trip of some 30 miles to Belfast by bicycle every day—and he had the added difficulty of working some unsocial hours. These circumstances called for a move to Belfast and under the Lord's overruling hand the family found a house in Fernwood Street, almost opposite to the Dunlops. Margaret at that time was just five. She remembers Nan, who was then sixteen, as a very jolly girl and well known by everyone in the street. The two families developed a very strong friendship.

The Williamsons belonged to the Congregational Church in Clifton Park Avenue, at the other side of Belfast, and they walked there to church every Sunday morning. However, it was impossible for Margaret and her younger sister Eileen to go back to Sunday School in the afternoon. Nan saw the opportunity and asked if Margaret could come to Sunday School with her. Mrs Williamson agreed, and Margaret started to come to Botanic Avenue. She liked it from the beginning and soon the whole family followed. A special bond grew up between Nan and Margaret Williamson and even when the Dunlops moved to University Avenue they continued to meet and often walked together. They maintained their contact when Nan went to India, and as we shall later see, their friendship was God's means of support at a time of particular trial. Reflecting in 1995 on Nan's Sunday School invitation and the attachment which matured from it, Mrs Leahy had this testimony: "Annie was always a missionary. She had a gift for seeing a need and had a great love for children. I had a great affection for her, and she had a profound influence on my life. In my family Annie was somebody special."

## Conversion and Indwelling Sin

Nan gave her life to Christ when she was twelve at a mission in Botanic Avenue church in November 1930, conducted by Rev H H Murphy. She understood her need of salvation and had been concerned about it. Her mother, in further testimony to her evangelical zeal, was always seeking to keep the children concerned. Rev Murphy's text was John 6:37 "Him that cometh unto me I will in no wise cast out."

When she was fifteen or sixteen Nan became aware of a problem with indwelling sin which affected her assurance of salvation. She did not understand the issue then as she came to understand it later. She knew she was a Christian, but she also knew that she was still a sinner. She never thought that she would feel like this after she was saved, and she was unable to reconcile the two things. She made the mistake of not speaking to anyone about it, not even to her mother. But she did pray about it and the Lord was her teacher. She prayed in the middle of the night and sometimes for quite a long time in the middle of the night. She was already thinking seriously about the mission field, but how could she go and tell others when she was still a sinner herself? She prayed kneeling at her own bed. Her sisters in the same room were younger—Lily, by seven years and Mary by five, but she did not disturb them. Jeannie was a later addition to the family.

One of the nights when she was praying, a picture came before her mind of a book and then of a hand wiping the book clean. The illustration was accompanied by the memory of Isaiah 44:22: "I have blotted out as a thick cloud, thy transgressions, and, as a cloud, thy sin: return unto me; for I have redeemed thee." "I never lost that," she says, "and I've been a sinner ever since." She prayed a lot about other things too, especially for the salvation of her brother Hugh, younger by a year. He joined the army as a peace-time soldier before the war, against the family's wishes, and was sent to India.

## Training and employment

Nan's first job on leaving school was in the local fancy linen industry with Irvine's in Adelaide Street. For various reasons God never allowed her to settle in a job until she began her life's calling, and her work as an embroideress in the linen business was the first example. Her own assessment of the few years she spent in it was simple: "I was quite hopeless at that. I took work home at nights and ripped out more than I sewed." How different from her missionary heroine, Mary Slessor, who achieved considerable skill in the textile trade! During those linen years Nan went to evening classes at Belfast Technical College and did some business training in shorthand, typewriting and book-keeping. She applied her book-keeping knowledge with appreciation when doing the orphanage and other accounts in her later years in India.

Later in her teens Nan talked to Rev W J Grier about her interest in the mission field and even proposed a particular Bible College to him—of which he disapproved. He advised nursing as a course which would not go amiss. So early in 1937 when she was eighteen, Nan applied to the Belfast Infirmary (later, Belfast City Hospital), sat the entrance exams, and was accepted. She commenced her training on 14th

August 1937. Student nurses then supplied their own uniform and were subject to three months' probation. The nurses slept in a dormitory and Nan was not ashamed to continue her practice of kneeling for prayer at her bedside when she moved into it. One of the girls threw a shoe at her and it was a Roman Catholic nurse who reproved her. Nan's witness encouraged other girls to pray like that too. The training was hard but she enjoyed it. She qualified as a State Registered Nurse in November 1940 and worked for some months as a 'charge nurse' until there was an opening for the one-year midwifery course.

Only those who passed their General examinations, preliminary and final, first time, were allowed to proceed to midwifery, and Nan was one of them. She started her training in the Spring of 1941, when "the Luftwaffe's tour of the ports" spread north to targets on the Humber, the Mersey and the Clyde, and to Belfast, with the heaviest blows in April and May. Belfast suffered three major attacks in which around 1000 people died during April and May. Nan was on the flat roof of Jubilee Maternity Hospital with some doctors on 'firewatching' duty when the Easter Tuesday raid took place on 15-16 April. The weather was clear for the first phases of the onslaught. Well over 100 aircraft attacked the city with hundreds of high explosive bombs and thousands of incendiaries, dropping flares on small parachutes to help them. The city's defences were ineffective. Many residential parts suffered direct hits with the result that about 750 people were killed and hundreds of others injured. "It was terrible," Nan recalled. "We could see the planes flying round and missing the shipyard. The place was lit up. Whole streets were wrecked, some not far from where we watched. They asked for volunteers to go across to the general hospital to help, and I went. People were searching for their relatives and sometimes finding them in the mortuary. A woman was brought in whose baby was being born when the bombs fell and half the roof caved in. The doctor threw himself across the baby, and the woman's mother across her. They lost everything but the woman said, 'I have my husband and my baby, so it's all right.'"

Nan completed her State Certified Midwife qualification in 1942 and was appointed a staff nurse. But there was to be no settling. Right on the heels of her appointment she was soon in one of the hospital beds herself for an appendicectomy. By this time her Nursing Superintendent, an English lady, had left to work with the forces, and Nan was not drawn to her replacement. The new Superintendent came over to the ward to see Nan who was suffering from paralytic ileus and other post-operative complications. There were electric fires on either side of her to keep her warm. "How are you today?" she enquired. "It has been very painful today," Nan said. "Well if you insist on having an operation you will have to put up with the pain of it!" Nan decided there and then that she would not be staying. Another Superintendent tried to persuade her to the contrary, but to no avail. They even asked her father to intervene, but he declined. Nan wrote her resignation, effective from 10th June 1942, on her return to work, with the Superintendent standing over her perhaps to ensure a non-critical letter, but Nan had no intention of making any point. So her career as a staff nurse in Belfast was short. But whatever we make of Nan's impulsive resignation from a good and useful position, its effect was that her roots again did not go down. Everything was to be temporary and preparatory until the Lord's plan for her could be put into effect.

Her next job was on the Grosvenor Road, in the Mulhouse munitions factory of Fairbairn Lawson Combe Barbour who were Contractors to the Admiralty and in association with Urquhart Lindsay and Robertson Orchar of Dundee. Mulhouse specialised in the manufacture of 25 pound shells. A member of the Botanic Avenue congregation ran a Nursing Agency which was also in Botanic Avenue. When one of the Mulhouse managers approached her for help in finding an industrial nurse, she directed him to Nan who had just left the City Hospital. She stayed with Mulhouse for about twelve months until the middle of 1943, as Welfare Supervisor, engaged in 'many and various duties' and taking charge of the ambulance room. It is fitting to quote from her testimonial: "She had a happy way of dealing with our workpeople with whom she was very popular but, when the occasion demanded it, she could be relied upon to be firm but tactful." As we shall see, her resignation was premature, but Nan was clear that the Lord wanted her to have the time of experience in treating industrial injuries. And He wanted her to have experience in another field too.

There were other strands to her preparation. When her interest in the mission field became established she heard of a teacher, probably through the local Christian Workers' Union, who gave very thorough tuition in English to intending missionaries. Nan had some very valuable lessons with her. The CWU is an inter-denominational body whose influence and usefulness was greatly increased as a result of the W P Nicholson campaigns. The organisation nurtured many of these converts, working through local mission halls where they held after-church services, weekly prayer meetings, and Sunday Schools. In addition they offered training. Nan attended one such training programme run by Miss Trenchard—an evening Christian Service Training Class. The students had to prepare papers and deliver them to the class for the others to offer criticism. Mr Grier similarly asked the young people to read papers at the Youth Fellowship. That was the sum total of her training. She also came to appreciate the training she received by listening to preaching in church. It came home to her once through an encounter with some Muslims in conversation. A man who was there asked, "How do you know all that?" Nan realised that a lot must have gone into her mind when Mr Grier was preaching, although she was not always consciously taking it in.

## The Growth of Missionary Interest

Among the Christian books Mrs Dunlop read to her children, Nan remembers the missionary lives of Mary Slessor and David Brainerd. In other books she introduced them to the Covenanters, the South American Indians and to children who were orphaned or had a difficult childhood for other reasons. Mrs Dunlop also sent Nan to 'The Sunrise Band', a children's missionary group which Lottie and Maisie McWilliam, members of the Lisburn Road congregation, held in their house. There they repeated Scripture verses from memory and prayed especially for children in Japan. Nan often took different children with her. Mrs Dunlop also provided a mission box for children who had never heard the gospel, and her own children were expected to put some pocket money into it. Her own missionary commitment was clear and sacrificial. At a particular missionary meeting when people were asked if they were willing to go themselves and parents if they were willing for their children to go, Mrs Dunlop signified her consent for her children. So Nan grew up in a missionary atmosphere. Missions and missionaries were always on the agenda. Her developing missionary call came through the need of people in foreign lands who were always before her mind. She made it clear to special friends even when she was about fifteen that she would be going to serve the Lord on the mission field.

But this general missionary call began to move in a specific direction. Nan started going to missionary meetings. Of those she attended one stands out in her memory as being of special significance in establishing her call. It was a meeting held by the Evangelical Union of South America in Belfast when she was sixteen. Slides were shown of the work and the whole thing left a deep impression on her. Her mother's choice of missionary reading meant that the need of South America was not new to her, but the EUSA meeting fixed it firmly in her mind. Other events and associations kept South America before her. In 1937 there were the murders of 'The Three Freds' in Brazil, which stirred considerable public interest and made an impression on Nan. One of the three was Fred Wright, a native of Belfast. Fred Wright's sister, Mrs Mary Blair, was a member of Botanic Avenue. So South America went on asserting itself. To go there, it seemed, she was definitely called.

**Meeting the Foreign Missions Committee**

When the time came for Nan to take some formal steps, Rev W J Grier directed her to the Free Church of Scotland, with whom the Irish Evangelical Church co-operated in foreign missions work. The church's first missionary, Dr Harold Lindsay, had been serving with the Free Church in Peru since 1938. Rev Joseph McCracken was now considering the mission in South Africa. Nan met the Foreign Missions Committee on 27 January 1943, after a rough and seasick crossing to Glasgow the night before. She spent her short time in Edinburgh with the family of Anne Rattray at their home on George IV Bridge. It is interesting to note in passing that Anne later married Rev Alvin Mackintosh, an Australian, who was studying at the Free Church College at the time of Nan's visit. Anne's mother was a close relative of Professor John Murray, and it was when he was staying in the same house in 1929 that he cabled Caspar Wistar Hodge with his acceptance of the call to Princeton Seminary, New Jersey. Nan's employers, Mulhouse, kindly gave her time off for her meeting with the Committee and did so again in May when she was presented to the Moderator of the Free Church of Scotland, Professor David Mackenzie, at the General Assembly.

During their introductory discussions the Committee presented to Nan the opportunities for medical service in both India and Peru. Nan had a firmly established momentum for South America, as we know, but at this point she signified her willingness, in principle, to serve in either. And as a measure of her commitment she offered to set out just as soon as her employers were able to replace her. She then withdrew while the Committee considered her application. India's need was pressing at this time in that Dr Annie Mackay was working without the support of a qualified nurse, and so the decision, which Nan heard on being recalled to the meeting, was to appoint her as a Missionary Nurse and to express the Committee's desire that she go to India. Over twenty years earlier Dr Annie Mackay had also expressed a preference for South America, where her brother Rev Calvin Mackay was serving in Peru, but she too was asked, and agreed, to go to India. Nan's interview was concluded with the agreement that the Committee would write to Nan, and to Rev W J Grier expressing their preference which she could then consider and give her formal response.

The Committee had asked her to go to *India*! Until the Committee meeting the last thing in Nan's mind had been to go to India. She was going to South America and had known it all along. India had never struck her as a mission field because India was *British* India. So it couldn't be a heathen land! She quickly acknowledged her strange misconceptions about a country of such vast need and cleared them away. In just a month she made up her mind and wrote to the Committee confirming that she would go to India. Mr Grier told her in a personal reference that if he were going to the mission field it would be to India or China that he would want to go. Perhaps that helped in her decision.

# 3

# To India—with a Little Ecumenical Help

**A Time to Wait**

The Committee met again on 3 March 1943 and received with gratitude Nan's acceptance for India. Two motions came before them. The first was that they should make Nurse Dunlop's acceptance known to the staff in India, inviting their response and their proposals with regard to her early commencement of work. The second motion was the direct route to the same result and was carried by a large majority— that the Committee accept Nurse Dunlop's offer, appoint her to India, and arrange for her to go.

The Committee meeting on 10 August 1943 brought to the agenda a problem which would not be easily or quickly resolved—a passage for Nan to Bombay in a time of war. On 21 October negotiations were proceeding with the Ministry of War Transport. By 16 November an application had been made for her passage, but no offer of one had been made. Another nine months passed before the subject came up again, and when it did, on 8 August 1944, expectation was dashed—a total ban had been placed on all overseas civilian travel. The Committee could only ask the clerk to enquire from the authorities about the prospect of the ban being lifted, and the period of waiting went on. But soon after that the situation began to change, and on 14

November 1944 the record states simply that Nurse Dunlop had sailed for India. The war in Europe was at its height.

One of the other items to appear among those minutes was the Committee's interest in providing some specialised medical training for Nan. But no course on tropical medicine could be found for her during the summer term of 1943. Another interesting note from November 1943 was that coupons for her outfit had been applied for and that her outfit allowance had been sent.

Not long after her Assembly visit in May 1943, Nan, believing that she would soon be on her way to India, left Mulhouse. But as the weeks went by with no news about her passage, she became perplexed about what to do. The army were crying out for nurses at the time. Nan began to consider it and told Mr Grier. He was clearly very annoyed. He said nothing at the time but wrote Nan a letter in which he placed before her the implications of a Christian "putting the hand to the plough and looking back." Nan was adamant that she was not looking back and that Mr Grier's Scriptural application on this occasion was wrong. But she did not proceed with her idea of army nursing and joined the Civil Nursing Reserve instead. Whether Mr Grier's application was right this time or not, his letter achieved the right decision and Nan acknowledged it. The Civil Nursing Reserve seconded her to a small maternity unit at Newtownards Hospital set up largely to accommodate Air Force wives. As the only midwife Nan got practical experience there which was of special relevance for her future work.

## On the Way at Last

On Wednesday morning 25 October 1944 Nan was in bed on sick-leave. She was having kidney investigations for low specific gravity, under the lady doctor who afterwards set up the renal unit in Belfast City Hospital. A telegram arrived for her which she assumed, as she opened it, was from the Civil Nursing Reserve, anxious about her return. In fact it was from the Foreign Missions Committee and was worded something like this: "We have a ship for your passage to India. Please be in Edinburgh on Friday." There was so much to be done in two days! Medical considerations were set aside. Nan went off to Newtownards and resigned. One of the house doctors told her that the obstetrician would be very sorry to lose her. She had championed the small Maternity Unit's cause and had seen its status grow. By now they had decided to build a new unit, "and he would just about put you in charge," the doctor said. "Well I'm not going in charge," Nan said, "I'm going to India."

She didn't think she needed much to take with her, but there were a few things she just had to get—and it was almost impossible to get anything because of the war. She had no passport, although she had applied for one. She needed a police permit to cross to Scotland in the first place. Mr Grier went out with her and she got the permit, along with a coat and a trunk. Her uncle worked in Anderson & McAuley, a leading Belfast department store, and he obtained a half set of white china for her. Mrs Sarah Patterson, one of the church members, helped her to get a pair of blankets from a shopkeeper she knew in Donegall Pass. The lady provided these without ration coupons, because her customer was going to the mission field. All Nan's possessions went into the new trunk. Along with it she had a small case as hand baggage which contained a dress, a skirt, a blouse, a cardigan, and a front for wearing with the cardigan.

Her quickly-arranged valedictory service was in her own home, now at 141 University Avenue, on the Thursday night. Members of the congregation came round after the Prayer Meeting. Mr Grier read a passage and spoke appropriately, and the church presented Nan with 'a packet of notes.' They sang Psalm 23 and commended her to the Lord in prayer. Nan's father, who felt her leaving very deeply, was unwell at the time, but he was able to be present and thanked the church for their support and their gift.

## The Passport

Nan set off for Edinburgh on Friday 26 October 1944 and on arrival she learned that she had to travel down to Liverpool. The Foreign Missions Committee entrusted her to the care of Dr Drummond, a Church of Scotland minister who was returning to India, and he accompanied her to Liverpool. She still had no passport. Dr Drummond went with her to the Passport Office who examined her file and asked for her birth certificate. Nan said, "You have it." But if they did it was a copy, for Nan found it on her first furlough, still at home in Belfast! When they told her that part of her papers were in Liverpool, part in London, and part in Belfast, it did not look promising. But Nan focused their minds with a deadline: "We have to be at the ship for 1 o'clock." And she concludes, "So we were at the ship for 1 o'clock—with the passport. How they gave me the passport I don't know, but the Lord wanted me to have it, and so it was." No doubt the presence of Dr Drummond was a big factor too. People at home were aware of the potential problem and some of them thought there was little hope of her sailing. Nan felt that the belief that she could soon be back made it easier for them to part.

## The War-Time Convoy

They moved out of Liverpool in convoy on Friday 3 November and went north to the Clyde, arriving the following day. They waited in cold, snowy weather for clearance until 6 November when they set sail for Port Said in convoy KMF 036 (Bombay). It was a convoy of 21 ships, with escort, and the first for some time to take civilians to foreign destinations. Rev and Mrs Joseph McCracken and their daugther Anne sailed for South Africa in one of its ships. Nan's ship, the *Stirling Castle*, was a vessel of the Union Castle Line which normally sailed only to destinations in Africa. There were 80 missionaries on board, about half of them ladies, sent out in groups by various church bodies—Irish Presbyterian, Church of Scotland, Anglican, and Roman Catholic. Nan was the only one without a denominational colleague, although a good friend of hers, Sadie Harrison, was in the Irish Presbyterian contingent.

The *Stirling Castle* had been converted for the use of troops and the lady passengers were accommodated in the reconstructed swimming pool area. Bunks were metal frames with canvas stretched across. The bathroom, designed for the use of troops, had a row of slate slabs housing hand-basins back to back with a cold tap between, so that two people faced each other as they washed. There were a couple of showers with a blanket for a door. The toilet doors were blankets too. Nan saw it all as good training and was quite happy with it all. And there were relative luxuries. The ship had a shop and they gave the passengers good food—far better food than was available at home. There were troops on the ship as well, and they did weapons training every day. The civilians had to do daily boat drill. There was one incident before leaving the south coast of England, when it felt as if the ship was being lifted out of the water. The passengers were informed that their escort had dropped six depth charges—but there must have been a reason for them to do so. Nan was sick during the voyage as well. While still at Glasgow, symptoms pointed once again to kidney problems. Later, a smallpox vaccination, for which there was no time before leaving, gave her a very sore arm.

Passing through the Straits of Gibraltar and along the Mediterranean Sea, the *Stirling Castle* completed the first leg of the journey to Port Said at the entrance to the Suez Canal. It sailed for Aden on 23 November, completing this second stage as an independent vessel, and on 28 November left Aden in convoy ABF 006, escorted by a submarine across the Arabian Sea to Bombay. The sea journey, with its zigzag course, took a month. Thankfully, there was no bad weather on that occasion. In spite of the Spartan conditions, the sickness, and the danger, Nan began her first letter home with the words: "I had a really lovely voyage."

**Bombay**

When the ship docked at Bombay on Monday 4 December 1944, the city was in a state of alert with anti-British rioting in support of India's demand for independence—an independence which was granted in August 1947. Nan's destination was Lakhnadon, near Jabalpur, some 600 miles north-east of Bombay, in the Central Provinces, and she thought it was just a matter of a transfer to the train. However, with the security situation as it was in Bombay, arriving passengers needed someone to take them off the ship, and because Nan had no-one to meet her she was not allowed to leave. There were three others in the same position. She could have disembarked with the Church of Scotland party and it was not long before she judged that this would have been the best option.

The next morning, Tuesday, she arranged with the Red Cross to send a wire to the mission superintendent, Rev Murray MacLeod, at Lakhnadon to tell him of her predicament and to ask for instructions, but it appears that that was not what the wire said. Mrs Sarah MacLeod tells the story as it unfolded to them: "Owing to war conditions we could not be informed about Miss Dunlop's sailing, and of course, we didn't know when she would arrive or at what port. So we had just to sit back and wait for her to take the first step. When the wire did come announcing her arrival at Bombay, Dr Mackay was at Chhapara, having been called out the day before, and we were out in camp ten miles from Lakhnadon! Although the wire arrived in Lakhnadon in the morning, Dr Mackay did not receive it until she came off the evening bus, and then she had to get it out to us! A man who was going out our way brought it, but it didn't reach us until 8.00 pm or 9.00 pm. What a rush we had next morning! Mr MacLeod hurried on by cycle to catch the first bus from Lakhnadon to Jabalpur. He wired a friend there to meet the train in case she arrived before he did. Meantime the children and I set off with the bullock cart." This was on Wednesday.

But had they known it, there was no hurry at the Lakhnadon end for Nan was still detained on board at Bombay. Of the three others left with her, two were Anglican missionaries from Dublin University— a lady doctor and a clergyman. They were going out for the first time. The other was a High Anglican Cambridge Brother, who had been out before. He belonged to 'The Society for the Propagation of the Gospel.' They would all be travelling with Nan as far as Jabalpur. At some point the authorities decided to solve the problem by putting them on the train to Jabalpur, but further delay was caused in obtaining a berth for Nan for the 24 hour journey. So it was Thursday when at last they were given a military escort across Bombay, put on the train, and told not to open the window. Murray MacLeod had already been waiting for 24 hours.

**And So To Lakhnadon...**

The trains at that time had windows of a triple construction. As well as the glass there was a shuttered device and behind that a very fine mesh net. Nan was amazed at the terrific noise at all the stations. People banged on the doors and the windows. They intended no harm. They just wanted in. The absence of language increased her sense of isolation and helplessness. Her travelling companions were very kind to her. After about 24 hours on the train, the Cambridge Brother, who knew the route, told Nan that they were now approaching Jabalpur. "What do I do?" she asked. "Take your baggage, get off, and go to the Station Master. Ask him to tell you where some missionary lives and just turn up at their door." Nan burst into tears. She felt that this was terrible. But he was very good—he just opened his book and conducted vespers as it was now evening. The lady doctor, sympathising much more with how Nan felt, said that if there was no one at Jabalpur to meet her she must continue her journey with them. They would then send to Lakhnadon for some one to come for her. But as we know, Rev Murray MacLeod had now been there for two days.

There was no bus to Lakhnadon until the next day so they stayed the night in Jabalpur with American Methodist missionaries. They started out on the last leg of the journey early the next morning, taking six hours to do the 53 miles. It was not at all what Nan had envisaged when she finally arrived in Lakhnadon around midday on Saturday 9 December 1944, 43 days after leaving Belfast. Her accommodation was not a Mary Slessor type mud house! It was the mission bungalow on the *Toriya* (little hill) compound, and a large, spacious room with a flagstone floor for her to sleep in. Dr Annie Mackay had placed the bed in the middle of the room, beautifully made up with a pink silk bedspread, and there were attractive curtains at the window. Nan had not realised when she packed her clothes in the trunk that they would be out of reach in the hold throughout the long journey. Getting hold of them again, along with her new surroundings and the warm welcome was a wonderful uplift. "After six weeks of my one dress and my one blouse and my one skirt and my one cardigan, I didn't know what was happening to me!"

Sarah MacLeod had planned an English meal for Nan as part of her welcome to Lakhnadon—but "the best laid schemes... !" Believing, as we know, that Nan would arrive on Thursday, she prepared an English midday meal. No doubt being even more confident about Friday, she did the same—but that exhausted her stock of English food. So Nan was welcomed with rice and lentils! Dr Annie Mackay said, "What will you do if she doesn't like that?" "Well, she'll just have to get to like it!" A lesson in contingency planning!

The crowning piece of the welcoming sequence was Rev Murray MacLeod's text the next day: "Nevertheless God, that comforteth those that are cast down, comforted us by the coming of Titus" (2 Cor 7:6). We do not know his points of application, but perhaps it was along the lines that whereas Titus brought comfort with him in the news he carried from Corinth, Nan was herself the news and the comfort it brought. Like Titus she had not turned up when expected, there had been an anxious time, but eventually they had the comfort of her safe arrival. Like Titus too she brought news of the love and zeal from a church removed by distance. Mr MacLeod had not yet had the opportunity to see in Nan something of the strength and toughness of Titus. He would not yet have known either, how fitting would become the eulogy to Titus, written by his successor in Crete, Cretensis, "The never silent trumpet of the evangelical message."

**4**

# Setting the Scene

What was this mission, based in two villages in the heart of India, to which Nan had come? How did it all begin? What stage of development had it reached when she arrived? What was this part of India like? What about the people, their customs, way of life, and religion?

### How it Began

The pioneer Free Church of Scotland missionary to Central India was Rev Stephen Hislop from Duns in Berwickshire. He went in 1844 to Nagpur, today in the state of Maharashtra, but at that time in the Central Provinces. He was a man with recognised expertise in a variety of fields including geology, botany, and administration, and he used the opportunities they gave him for the Gospel. He went on regular evangelistic tours into the provinces, but following the pattern of Dr Alexander Duff during the previous fifteen years in Calcutta, he developed Christian education as the core activity of his missionary strategy. He was drowned in 1863 in a swollen stream when returning at night to Nagpur when he was just 46, after an extremely fruitful and influential ministry. 'Hislop College' in Nagpur still bears witness to his memory.

A few years later, in 1871, the Free Church of Scotland handed over the northern part of its Nagpur

based work—the Seoni area, located between Nagpur and Jabalpur—to the Original Secession Church.
This was the remnant of a body which had left the
Church of Scotland in 1733, and who, in the late
1860's, were expressing interest in working in Central India. They began to send missionaries immediately of whom the most notable was Rev John
McNeel, an American, who went in 1898. In the
'Union' of 1900, a large majority of the Free Church
of Scotland joined with other Presbyterian bodies to
form the United Free Church of Scotland. All the
Free Church missionaries, including those in Central
India joined the new body, the United Free Church,
effectively separating the Free Church from all its
foreign missions. Greatly reduced in size and resources as it was, the Free Church was nevertheless
determined to continue its witness overseas, and in
India it directed support to the work of the Secession
church at Seoni. Dr Jeannie Grant from Glenurquhart
Free Church joined the Secession mission in 1901
and remained in service with it until her death in
1953.

In 1905 a Free Church Biblewoman, Miss Elizabeth MacLeod, joined the work at Seoni, and the
two churches made another agreement—this time
that the Free Church would take over the northern
part of the Seoni work from the Secession Church as
soon as it was possible. This part was the area under the local government of Lakhnadon. When Dr
Annie Mackay joined Miss Macleod in 1921, the Free
Church took steps to implement the agreement and
resume its own mission. It made known the need for
a minister to lead the work, and as a result, Rev
Evan Mackenzie, previously a Church of Scotland
missionary in Tibet, and his wife Eva, were appointed. They commenced work in Lakhnadon in

Service in a Sari

1924. In the following year Miss MacLeod and Dr Mackay moved from Seoni to Chhapara, a village seventeen miles to the south of Lakhnadon. So the Free Church re-opened its work some 120 miles north of its original Nagpur base, but within the same territory, and after a break of nearly 25 years. The Free Church and Secession missions co-operated to the full in their neighbouring regions. John McNeel and his family gave invaluable practical help and wise counsel to successive Free Church missionaries including Nan Dunlop. Nan, and one of John McNeel's daughters, Mary, also a missionary nurse, became life-long friends.

## The Field, its People, and Religion
The mission field throughout the years of its existence has been the area of 1600 square miles, with its 800 villages, coming under the regional jurisdiction of the Lakhnadon courts. This is an area about the size of Caithness in Scotland or half the size of County Antrim in Northern Ireland. It is part of the Seoni District, in the state of Madhya Pradesh (Central Provinces), India's largest state. The language is *Hindi*, the official language of India. It is in the northern tropics, and has a wet and dry tropical climate with January temperatures of 70°-80° (21°-27°C), but soaring to 120° (49°C) in May and early June. The monsoons come between mid-June to September, followed by the coolest period of the year, October to February. Most of the people are villagers and have their employment mainly in livestock and crop farming— wheat, lentils, rice, mustard seed, oil seed, peanuts and soya beans. The rice harvest is in October and the wheat harvest in February. The women collect wood from the jungle to help finance their family needs.

The majority people in the Lakhnadon area are *Gondhs*—one of India's aboriginal groups. They often live in their own Gondh villages, though they have lost their Gondh language. They are animists, believing that spirits live in trees, rocks and similar things, but have become progressively influenced by Hinduism. There is also a minority *Muslim* representation in the region. Sometimes it is the Muslims who are the landowners and the heads of villages, especially around Chhapara.

The dominant religion is Hinduism with its belief in *Reincarnation*—the soul does not die but goes on being reborn, in human or in animal life. The process is governed by the law of *Karma*—a belief that every action, great or small, influences the quality of the next rebirth. As polytheists they worship various divinities and animals too—mainly the cow. They have a ranking system of social classes or *castes* which often correspond with different occupations. For example, Chhapara means 'six parts', its name deriving from the caste background. The caste system and its distinctives are less pronounced today, especially in the cities.

* * * * * * *

To see the full picture of the mission as it was at the end of 1944, when Nan arrived, we need to look at its several distinct but inter-dependent elements—accommodation, medical work, the care of orphans, Christian education, church work and evangelism. It is important also that we try to visualise the two villages in which the work of the whole field was centred—Lakhnadon and Chhapara. We begin with them.

## Lakhnadon and Chhapara

These two villages are located in an area of hilly table-
land in the foothills of the Satpura mountains. They
stand about 2000 feet above sea level with
Lakhnadon slightly higher than Chhapara. Chhapara is
situated on the banks of the Wainganga river. The
appearance of the countryside changes a good deal
with the seasons. The heat of summer leaves it barren
and burnt, but at other seasons 'flame of the forest'
trees and a few date palms are in evidence along with
the wide variety of crops. The attractive mango trees
stay green throughout the year and produce their fruit
in the hot season. After the rains there are rivers,
rivulets and streams flowing among the hills. Landowners build *bunds* or embankments on sloping
ground to keep the rain water from escaping into
someone else's land. Teak is grown commercially on
the surrounding hills, turning the whole area into what
is known as *jungle*. The livestock in the fields are
mostly cows, buffalo and goats, often undernourished
and skinny. Darkness falls early and quickly, around
7.00 pm in the summer and 5.00 pm in the winter.
This was Nan's new environment, and many of the
features have not altered in the half century since she
first took it all in.

What were the villages themselves like when Nan
first arrived? The population of Lakhnadon was around
3000 and Chhapara more like 5000. The women
dressed in the s*ari*, a length of material measuring five
or six metres by one metre, draped round the body
like a long dress, the loose end going over the head or
shoulder. The material could be silk, cotton or nylon.
Local men wore the *dhoti*, a simple garment wrapped
around the waist and between the legs to form loose
trousers. Magistrates and other officials had a preference for Western dress. The policemen wore khaki

shorts and and shirts, and did drill every morning out-side the station. Very often the smaller children had a type of loincloth only, with nothing underneath, and this cut down the need for washing!

The men and women were employed mainly on the land, working with livestock, planting and harvest-ing crops, and general farm labouring. Both men and women broke 'road metal' or stone for the Govern-ment road projects too. They worked with hammers at the side of the road breaking pieces of stone into smaller grades to be used as a bed for the road sur-face. They were paid per pile of stones. Then they dug the mud from the roadside with pickaxes and carried it in baskets on their heads to spread on top of the 'road metal.' The roller followed to compact the surface.

The shops in the village bazaar were open-fronted. There were no windows of course, only a rough shut-ter at closing time. There were no footpaths either; shoppers just stepped up from the road into the shop as though stepping into someone's hall. The streets were quite narrow in Lakhnadon with a trench dug along the side for drainage, rubbish, and worse. The public toilets were an open piece of waste ground, but often those trenches at the side of the streets served the same purpose. A flagstone across the trench was the stepping stone from the road to the houses or shops. The owners lived at the back or upstairs—if there was an upper storey. Chhapara was different in some respects with its much wider bazaar, and its shops on each side. It was better for shopping than Lakhnadon. There were cloth shops, pots and pans shops, food shops. Fruit and vegetable sellers came in from the country and sold their produce at stalls. An-other feature of the villages was the *mohallas*, or separate caste quarters. The silversmiths, for example, lived in their own *sonari mohalla* where they crafted and sold necklaces, bracelets, anklets, and icons. The community of leather workers did the same in the *chhamari mohalla*. There were goldsmiths, water carriers, sweepers, and so on.

Tiny village houses made up the rest. Sometimes they were very tiny—not much more than two or three metres square. Nearly all of them had an area at the front which, like the floor inside, was plastered by hand with cow dung. Around it was a ledge where people could sit and rest. At the back there might have been a verandah where more often than not the cows took shelter from the heat or the rains. The family cooking was done on the back verandah too. Inside there was usually an alcove in the wall which displayed the family's gods—and they were a people of "gods many and lords many." The family slept on the floor on mattresses or bundles of cloth which they stored to one side during the day. The baby's cot was a hammock slung across the middle of the room.

## The Mission Accommodation

What about the places where the missionaries lived and from which they worked? In 1924 when the Free Church had decided to resume its own missionary work in the Lakhnadon area, Rev John McNeel of Seoni helped with the purchase of a fifteen acre field less than a mile from the village. However, when Rev Evan Mackenzie arrived later that year, he decided instead that the mission would be better situated on a hill, for the benefit of health and to give the work the advantage of visual prominence. A hill location of five acres, ten minutes' walk away from the fifteen-acre field obtained by John McNeel, was given to the mission and the first buildings were erected. The site became known as the *Toriya* (the little hill). The hospital was afterwards built on the fifteen-acre field. Evan

Mackenzie had ambitious plans for a complex of buildings on the *Toriya*, but poor health forced him to resign in 1927. Lakhnadon has expanded over the years and today the *Toriya* is part of a built-up area.

The work in Chhapara, seventeen miles to the south, was based in the village itself. When Dr Annie Mackay and Miss Elizabeth Macleod arrived from Seoni in December 1925, they rented an upstairs room in a Muslim home of good standing in the centre of the village. Before long they were able to move to a small house of their own towards the edge of the village and nearer the main road. This house had been used by evangelists from Seoni, and John McNeel, who had built it, superintended its renovation. It had three rooms, a bedroom each for the two ladies, with a dining/sitting room between. Murray Macleod added a fourth room on the end when he and his family lived in Chhapara in the forties. When Nan moved to Chhapara in 1945 it was Miss Macleod's room which became hers. Today, the bungalow is part of the 'mission compound', and is divided into 'flats' which are owned by the later mission orphans. Dr Annie and Miss Elizabeth worked together until 1944, when Miss Elizabeth retired, covering both Lakhnadon and Chhapara, and dealing with every aspect of the work between them. Dr Annie was usually located in Lakhnadon from 1928, making weekly visits to Chhapara.

**The Medical Work**

Turning next to the medical work, it is appropriate to start with Chhapara, for it was there that it began with the arrival of Dr Annie and Miss Elizabeth in 1925. They did medical and dispensary work during the day on the ground floor verandah of the Muslim-owned house where they had rented accommodation.

They later moved the dispensary to a small house in the goldsmiths' quarter near the shopping bazaar, which, with John McNeel's help once again, they adapted for its new function. Further adapted in 1957, it served the community for more than 55 years.

Switching to Lakhnadon, we pick up the medical story with Dr Willie Urquhart, who came to the village in 1926. At first he used a travelling dispensary which Rev Evan Mackenzie had recommended. He towed it as a caravan behind the car and took it to villages where the car could go. Dr Urquhart also worked from the *Toriya*. Sadly, he too suffered poor health, and had to return home in 1930. But 1934 marked a significant step for the future of the medical work. Before leaving Scotland after furlough that year, Dr Annie pleaded for a small hospital, "even with only five beds." Her plea was like seed that fell on good ground, for funds were provided, and in 1936 Lakhnadon Hospital was built. Dr Jeannie Grant from Seoni, cut the tape and declared it open. Nan became its first nursing recruit. The hospital did not replace the existing arrangements—the staff continued their medical outreach to villages and homes.

**Orphan Care**

Here again there is an important link with Seoni and the work of John McNeel. The Seoni orphanage grew quickly between 1900 and 1920 as parents died through famine and epidemics. When Dr Jeannie Grant joined the Seoni mission in 1905, Free Church congregations in Scotland began to adopt individual orphans. About a year after Evan and Eva Mackenzie arrived in Lakhnadon in 1924, they opened their door to three children of one family and cared for them for eighteen months until the Seoni courts removed them. These children had not been legally adopted, and Hindu opponents, seeing their opportunity, achieved a significant victory. The other early missionaries, Dr Willie Urquhart and Rev Murray Macleod, also argued for the establishment of an orphanage, but the Foreign Missions Committee, concerned about the uncertain future of the work in India and the possibility of further Hindu legal action, felt unable to comply. They did not however forbid the care of individual children.

The discretion allowed to missionaries to care for individual children in certain circumstances, developed a *de facto* orphanage situation, albeit small, and it began to look inevitable that Foreign Missions Committee policy was bound to change accordingly. But it was not until 1955 that the orphanage was given official status. In 1932 the mission legally adopted two girls, Jaiwanti, an infant, and Surajmukhi who was about ten. In 1934 Prakash Kumar arrived, and in 1938, Alexander John. By 1940, ten children were in care. The children lived on the Lakhnadon *Toriya* until 1951 when they were moved to Chhapara, although a few of them had already gone there to attend the school. Mrs Gajaribai Lall was employed to look after the children during the *Toriya* years and her daughter, Tarabai, a Nursery School Teacher, provided their early education.

**Christian Education**

The school began in Chhapara in 1901 as yet another initiative of John McNeel of Seoni. It took a big step forward in 1905, when a local headman gifted land with a new building, and Primary and Middle schools were formally opened. More encouragement came in 1930 with a new Middle school in a purpose-built building, but the Foreign Missions Committee in Edinburgh felt obliged to close it in 1940 because of a shortage of qualified staff. The Primary school then moved into the building. During her years in Chhapara, Elizabeth Macleod was Manager of the school, a role in which Nan followed her later. Christian teaching was always part of the curriculum. The school has continued to occupy the same site and has flourished. Today it has Nursery, Primary, and Middle sections with over 800 pupils. Alexander John, one of the early orphans, is Headmaster.

Lakhnadon provided the teaching for the orphan children on the *Toriya* during the 1930's and 40's until they were ready for school in Chhapara. When the Middle School closed in 1940, they went away to Boarding Schools run by other Missionary Societies. Education resumed at Lakhnadon in 1994 with the opening of a new Primary Mission School on the *Toriya*.

## Church and Evangelism

With the church side of the work we think first of the Salve family of Lakhnadon, the only Indian family to maintain a Christian witness there since the 1920's. It was Mr Salve, senior, who helped Evan Mackenzie find temporary accommodation on his arrival in 1924 and who later arranged for the purchase of a site for the church near the Lakhnadon bazaar. Worship was held in the Salves' home and on the *Toriya* before the church was opened. The other early helper was Mr Laxman Forbes who was an evangelist with the mission from 1924. He afterwards lived beside the hospital.

Rev Murray Macleod and his wife Sarah, a trained nurse, arrived in Lakhnadon in 1933. Based first in Lakhnadon and later in Chhapara he ministered widely around the villages. He lived with his family in one of them, Sahajpuri, for two years. It was he who organised the building of the church in 1935 on the site acquired by Mr Salve, and in 1944 when Nan arrived he was the Superintendent of the mission. He was noted for his exceptional gift in speaking the Hindi language, and as a preacher he was in great demand at conferences all over India. He and his family will feature in our story as it progresses. In Chhapara, for the first five years, the church worshipped on the verandah of private homes or in the small school building of 1905. From 1930 the services were transferred to the new school.

The missionaries and their Indian colleagues did not carry out evangelism separately from the other work of the mission, but integrated it with everything they did. They evangelised while dispensing medicines, in the hospital waiting room, and as part of the village visits. They preached in the open-air, visited local Hindu festivals, and distributed Bibles, Gospels, Scripture portions and Christian literature. They organised evangelistic camps and children's camps. They held Sunday Schools and Children's Meetings. They brought up the orphans as the children of Christian families. Trained local evangelists and Biblewomen shared the work with the missionaries, often with great faithfulness. In some cases they were also trained to carry out basic medical care and procedures, and this they combined with their witness. During the rains when work at the villages was suspended, Murray Macleod gathered them together for study and theological instruction.

It is interesting that during the hot weather they sometimes evangelised at nights, since the terrific heat made it impractical to go to villages and bazaars through the day. Rev Murray Macleod, writing in 1938 about village work in April, gives us this account: "After the prayer meeting this evening I spoke to the *Babus* (the men) about going at night to a nearby village. They said they had meant to approach me with the same suggestion. After dinner, therefore, we set out for the little village on the outskirts of Chhapara, named Tinsa... . Having sung one or two *bhajans*, Babu Forbes spoke to them on sin and the sinner's need. Babu Prem followed, bringing before them God's plan of salvation, and in conclusion I spoke to them on the appropriation of God's love-gift by faith. Here again we found the reception most encouraging. The people seemed glad to hear and anxious to understand. They asked us to tell them beforehand when we intended to return so that all might be present."

\* \* \* \* \* \* \*

This, then, was the situation to which Nan arrived in December 1944. Miss Elizabeth
Macleod had retired earlier that year and returned to Scotland. So had Miss Lena Gillies who had served since 1930. Edith and Anna Stewart, also missionaries of the 1930's, had each married and was working with her husband's mission. There remained only Dr Annie Mackay in Lakhnadon, and in Chhapara, Murray and Sarah Macleod who were not to stay long-term. There was much that was beautiful and challenging as Nan settled in and took stock. There were elements of excitement. But difficulties abounded. The hospital was primitive. The climatic conditions were a trial. She faced times of loneliness. Above all, the people were spiritually in great darkness. It was all too obvious that the task was enormous, resources small, and the opposition great. But Nan had a great God. And she believed Him.

**5**

# The First Year

As we pick up the threads of the story again, we recall that when Nan arrived in India on Monday 4 December 1944, the Mission Superintendent, Rev Murray Macleod and his family were away at a village camp ten miles from Lakhnadon. On receiving Nan's wire from Bombay they hurried back to Lakhnadon on the Wednesday, but as we also know, Nan's arrival was delayed until Saturday. They spent the Saturday and Sunday together on the *Toriya*, and on Monday Nan left her pleasant bedroom behind and joined the family, as they returned, partly by bullock-cart, partly on foot, to camp. A bullock-cart or *chakra*, in Hindi, was a two wheel cart with no springs and Sarah Macleod gives us some insight into this mode of travel as she describes the journey from camp to Lakhnadon in the previous week: "... as the path to the main road was so rough and stony, we preferred to walk the three miles. Being tossed about in the cart all the time, it was impossible to manage our precious can of milk! Alistair (their son) wouldn't wait for the cart, so he went ahead. He walked and ran the whole ten miles, arriving hours before us! Morrison (their other son) walked six miles, and I picked him up later with a cut knee. I jogged along about two miles an hour, cramped up in the cart, with the sun beating down." And this was the winter sun!

## A Village Camp

So Nan began her missionary service at a village camp under canvas, with its very basic amenities. These evangelistic camps, which usually lasted about six weeks, were held during the winter months, November - February, when the monsoons had passed and the lower temperatures made outdoor work possible during the day. The missionaries and Indian Christians worked together preaching and distributing Christian literature. They also provided simple medical care, attending daily to patients who arrived. The programme included visits to other villages in the locality of the camp site, which they reached on foot, by bullock-cart, or by bicycle— whichever was most appropriate.

Nan met Godwin Laxman at this first camp. He was the son of one of the early Seoni orphans, cared for by Rev John McNeel, and had become an evangelist with the mission. He had also been trained to dispense a range of medicines. Godwin gave Nan her first Hindi lessons at that camp and she found it not too bad. Soon she realised that she could speak the language more easily than she could read or write it. At that camp she also treated her first patients, with Alistair Macleod helping to interpret.

## Language - A Weapon of War!

Although Nan, as the hospital's first nursing recruit, was based at Lakhnadon during her initial eleven months, it is interesting to note how little time she was able to spend there. This was primarily due to the precedence which language study took over everything else. Sarah Macleod, conscious of the war-awareness on the part of readers at home in 1945, made the case like this: "In **our** war language study must have 'priority rights.'" There were no facilities at Lakhnadon, but the two Christian teachers at the school in Chhapara were well qualified to do it. So, for the first few months, Nan took the bus to Chhapara and stayed with the Macleods from Monday to Friday each week, going back to spend the week-ends with Dr Annie in Lakhnadon. The two Chhapara teachers each gave her three quarters of an hour's language study every day, and Murray Macleod added an hour of basic grammar in the evenings. When she was not engaged in study she worked in the dispensary and cared for the orphans who had moved from Lakhnadon for schooling. This early association with Chhapara proved providential in determining Nan's future sphere of service. Chhapara was soon to become her home for almost the entirety of her missionary career.

Turning again to one of Sarah Macleod's early letters we get a glimpse of a typical bus journey from Lakhnadon to Chhapara in 1945: "Miss Dunlop, like all the others of us, has to travel by bus. Last Monday she had to wait hours for one. When it did come it was packed, and the driver, knowing that she didn't know Hindi, tried to overcharge her, but she was quite a match for him! She took back the rupee note which she had given and counted out the correct amount in change! She couldn't get a seat, and as no-one offered her one, she had to sit on the floor all the way to Chhapara."

In May 1945 Nan went for two months to Language School in Landour, near Dehra Dun, 500 miles north of Lakhnadon-Chhapara, and 6000 feet up in the foothills of the Himalayas, where it was pleasantly cool. The Macleods were there too, as Murray Macleod was conducting Bible studies for more than 70 missionaries of various nationalities and denominations. During her stay Nan had her first experience of an earthquake. No damage was done, but the house shook in a way that reminded her of the Luftwaffe's blitz of Belfast four years before. In the short time since her arrival in India, Nan had made good progress in speaking and even reading the language, but found the more formal grammar studies at Language School a different proposition. She started in the top class, but had to drop down a grade because of it. And her old problem with spelling re-asserted itself too! She recorded in a letter from Landour: "I am finding the language difficult, very difficult, and I want to try to sit for the examinations in September, instead of waiting until March. Please make that a very definite matter of prayer. I can't do much without the language, and I want very much to work among the children."

In fact Murray Macleod decided that Nan should wait until March to sit her first year Hindi exams. She willingly accepted the wisdom of it: "... for if at the beginning one does not get a proper grounding in grammar, then later on it is more difficult. I know myself that even if I had passed, as my pundit (Brahman Hindu Teacher) said I would, still I had no firm grasp of things. Since I returned Mr Macleod has given me great help and explained things in a way the pundits never did. I now feel more confident, and can stumble through a few parables in my own words." As we shall later see, Nan developed quite an exceptional gift with Hindi, including the local dialects.

## A Hospital with a Difference

In the modish jargon of the 1990's we only get one chance at a first impression. Well, Lakhnadon Hospital, opened with five beds just eight years before, made a lasting first impression on Nan, the first of its nursing recruits. In her first letter home, 17 December 1944, she described it like this: "Things are rather different from what I expected with regard to the hospital. It is really still pioneer work—a sort of dispensary work—that is at present being done. The hospital building is there all right, but it still needs to be put into going order, and that will not be an easy matter, as many of the patients who do come bring the whole family and will not go into bed; they just throw a heap of dirty rags on the floor and sit there, go outside, light a fire, and cook their meals. The main difficulty is caste; they won't even take a drink of water from us; so what are we to do? Then most of the diseases are rather different from what we get at home. Dr Mackay has done a great deal single-handed; she works very hard indeed, and she feels she will be able to do a lot more now that she has a nurse; but what is one nurse towards helping to establish a proper hospital? I feel so insufficient, and I know that the prayers of the people at home can do a great deal more than they realise."

Within a few months Nan's letters were giving a more complete picture of the hospital work with references to its very busy schedules as patients arrived day after day, some requiring major surgery. There were four small wards at that time which could accommodate two beds each, but always more patients than the hospital could care for, with accompanying relatives in addition. The Outpatients consulting room had four other rooms opening off it—a laboratory, a store, a dressing room and a waiting room where the patients and their families were presented with the Gospel as they waited to see the doctor. Too often they seemed to pay no real attention even though many of them knew the story well. The dispensary staff in Outpatients then were two ladies—Tarabai and Ruthbai. 'Bai' is the Hindi word for 'woman' and is used in central India as a term of respect. Dr Annie had trained them to dispense. Tarabai was also the teacher of the orphans living on the *Toriya*. Ruthbai was the daughter-in-law of Mr Salve of Lakhnadon, the Indian Christian who had identified with the mission from its beginning. These ladies working together dispensed the medicines which Dr Annie was busy prescribing in the consulting room, did the dressings, and evangelised. One of them would always be behind the dispensary counter, and the other speaking to the people. The patients normally paid a reasonable amount for medicine as Dr Annie considered that this would make them value it more.

## A Missionary Doctor

It is appropriate at this point to outline a day in the life of Dr Annie Mackay with whom the other missionaries were so closely bound up. Nan describes her simply as a wonderful person, absolutely imperturbable, and who never caused a fuss about anything. First thing in the morning she attended to various duties on the *Toriya*. The animals needed daily attention. These were the bullocks which pulled the *chakra*, and the buffalo which drew the water from the well below the hospital up to the tank on the *Toriya*. She supervised the provision of their fodder, and the maintenance of their ropes and harness. Then she arranged the children's food. There were about ten orphans at that time. The grain which provided their basic diet was grown in a field at the bottom of the hill and kept in a store off Nan's room. After these tasks were completed, she went down the hill to the hospital, and for the rest of the morning did her rounds and saw the patients at the daily outpatients' clinic. Lunch and a half hour rest followed.

In the afternoon Dr Annie went off on her bicycle into Lakhnadon village where she combined medical work with opportunities for evangelism. On the way back she stopped at the hospital and did her evening rounds. In addition she may well have had a call-out, perhaps on a maternity case. If she was needed at the hospital when she was up on the *Toriya* the man who looked after the *chakra*, who lived in the hospital grounds, put out a white sheet to let her know. On a normal evening she would come back up the hill around 6 o'clock, bath, and get ready for the evening meal. Nan recalls that she wore a long dress at this time of the day, for protection against the mosquitoes, as much as anything else. Nan very soon copied her. Dr Annie would then sit for a time, knit for the children and conduct family worship. Finally she went through to her room and did the accounts. She also visited Chhapara every Tuesday and at other times when the need arose. This was her very full day—six days a week.

### Stories of the First Year

Nan believes that she was the first of the lady missionaries to wear the *sari*, starting just a few months after her arrival. This would of course have been on occasions when she was not wearing her white hospital uniform. She also wore a *topi*, a khaki coloured sun hat, when she first arrived, but she didn't care for it, and with her change to the *sari* it became unnecessary in any case. She remembers the first time she went out in her *sari* in Chhapara. The Patail, the head of the village and the son of the man in whose house Dr Annie and Miss Elizabeth had rented accommodation when they first arrived in 1925, met

Nan on the road and immediately registered his approval of the change: "Very nice now," he remarked, "Don't be coming out in your petticoat again!"

It was not long before Nan had a taste of illness, brought on by local conditions. It was septicaemia. She had had some bad mosquito bites which were aggravated by prickly heat—an itchy rash which occurs in hot humid conditions. Sleeping outside, where it was cooler, she would pour cold water all over herself and rub with kerosene oil to take the itch away. Inevitably she scratched one of the bites which afterwards became infected during a delivery. She was so ill that Dr Annie asked Tarabai, who had very little English then, to sleep in her room with her. During the night Nan rigored badly and Tarabai called Dr Annie because she thought Nan was shivering with cold. But her temperature registered over 104°. Dr Annie was worried. She prescribed M&B 693 sulphonamide tablets, which was the only remedy then, but Nan was unable to swallow them until the next day. Her condition improved a little over the next day or two, but her leg was still black and Sarah Macleod, also a nurse, warned her not to get out of bed. But Nan did, and then was unable to make it back from the bathroom. Mrs Macleod, who evidently enjoyed plain speaking when the occasion required it, said: "I told you not to get out of bed, so you can get back into it the way you got out of it!" She put fomentations on the infected area which felt so hot that Nan, who could also speak quite plainly, told her: "If you lift the skin off it, maybe you'll be happy then!" Nan was not allowed to see her leg at first but when she did, she got out of bed and plunged it into a bucket of water. This was of course contrary to her nurse's specific wishes, but what is one nurse's opinion against another! Nan got septicaemia twice, but simply commented: "You just got over those things."

All of the Lakhnadon community understandably did not accept the missionaries very readily in those early years although they were usually willing to come to them for help. This could make it difficult if anything went wrong and Nan had some very unhappy experiences in her first year. The first baby she delivered in Lakhnadon village was mentally subnormal, and the people considered that their involvement with the missionary midwife was to blame. Consequently they would not call Nan again, although she did not find out the reason until the local government doctor told her. His wife was expecting a baby and the people had warned him to avoid Nan. However, the doctor did call her, but as she set to work she very quickly realised that unless God helped her in a special way there would be another unhappy ending and the people confirmed in their misgivings. It was a very difficult breech presentation and when Nan later looked back on her life's work as a missionary midwife, she could not remember a delivery of such complication. But baby boy and mother both survived. The magistrate who lived next door to the doctor was the next to call her. His first wife had died in childbirth just after the doctor who delivered her had left. This time everything went well and Nan delivered a baby boy. Soon after, she delivered the wife of a forestry officer and that too went well—another boy.

Triplets were born just at that time too, with Nan in attendance. They were all boys and healthy, but as triplets they were unwanted—and the presence of a missionary midwife was not without significance for what had happened, in the eyes of some who were present. They put the babies into a *soupa,* a

## Service in a Sari

woven winnowing sieve, and simply left them on the floor to die. Nan asked the government doctors to intervene, and then offered to take the babies herself, but the family declined the request.

Another case concerned a woman belonging to a family of silversmiths in Chhapara who had just had her third still-birth. Her symptoms suggested some form of severe post-natal depression and she was in a pretty bad state. Nan could only comfort her, talk to her, and show her kindness, but the woman responded to it and was restored to a good measure of calm and stability. The family were so impressed and appreciative that they invited Nan to come and speak to them. She was still struggling with the language at that stage and asked Murray Macleod to do it for her. But he declined, taking the view that Nan was ready for the challenge and its opportunities herself. He was right. When she arrived to give her talk she found the whole family gathered, all of them in their best clothes, showing the importance and respect they attached to the occasion. Through this Nan formed a lasting friendship with them. The woman had another baby which Nan delivered, and named it *Awinash*—'Indestructible.' Sadly, the following year, this baby also died. Nan was away on holiday, but such was the confidence of the family in her that they believed the baby would not have died had she been there. On another occasion, when one of the men of the family died, they sent Nan a wire saying 'Your brother has died.' The woman had other children, and the friendship continued, but so far as we know, no members of that family believed.

Then there were the language gaffes! One day Nan was called to a woman who had a retained placenta which Nan removed. Dr Annie was away at the time. Nan's Hindi was still not very good, and

60

the next day people came from the woman's family, mentioning her by name and talking about collapse. Nan dropped everything at the dispensary, got on her bicycle, and taking with her what she could in the bag, pedalled to the woman's house "like fury." In fact it was the woman's husband who had collapsed. He had typhoid, and just when she had given him the appropriate medicine, his own government doctor arrived. Nan apologised to him for treating his patient, but he was very good about it and there was nothing to worry about.

There was another incident towards the end of her first year at a stage when Nan had become more confident with the language. She had learned the names of the various family relationships as this was important in Indian culture, and when a woman came and called her for her *bahinowi* Nan was quite sure she was talking about her sister-in-law, for the Hindi word for sister is *bahin*. Arriving at one of the tiny houses she found a tall man lying on the floor, and as the room was so small his feet were sticking out through the door. It was the woman's brother-in-law. Nan took a fit of laughing which upset the woman, and Nan did not have the Hindi to explain what was so funny. But the man recovered, and the woman brought Nan two eggs to express her thanks.

There was one really unpleasant encounter of another kind. Nan's bedroom, the one on the *Toriya* at Lakhnadon, which gave her such a lift when she arrived, had a bathroom 'en suite' — in a manner of speaking. There was an enamel basin on a round metal stand for washing and then there was a low brick enclosure, against an outside wall, a bit like a shower tray, for a standing bath. A bath consisted in pouring water with a hand jug from large earthenware pots standing within arm's reach. The water ran out through a hole in the wall. But what lets out lets in, and one day after bathing Nan discovered a snake curled up behind her towel rail. It was an unpleasant shock, but this one, unlike another some years later, thankfully did her no harm.

## A Little Diversion

Edith and Anna Stewart, two sisters who went to the Indian field in 1935 and 1938 respectively, both married missionaries there, each within about three years of arriving. They continued to serve in India, but their move to other work created a little sensitivity which Nan enjoys referring to as it came to rest on herself. She had her first touch of it when addressing the Women's Foreign Missions Association at the 1943 Assembly in Edinburgh. Several of the ladies spoke to her about the Stewart girls, lamenting their loss to the mission, and hoping that the same thing would never, never happen again! Nan responded, "Well, you know the remedy. Send out a few men!" And in telling the story half a century later, she added, "Which they didn't do!"

At the time Nan was leaving for India her photograph appeared in the *Monthly Record,* the Free Church of Scotland's church magazine. Not long after her arrival on the field she received a letter from a young man in Scotland. He told her about himself, his sister and his home and went on to express his interest in the Indian field. He asked Nan to write to him. She brought the letter to the family table, and announced the news that a young man was interested in India. Murray Macleod said, "Let me have it. I'll answer that." And Nan reflected, "That's the last I saw of the letter!"

## The Orphan Scene

What about the orphans in that first year, and Nan's role in caring for them? There were ten of these children in 1940 and the number grew slightly in the following years. We noted earlier in the story that during the 1930's and the 1940's they lived in small houses on the *Toriya* behind the main mission bungalow, before education and accommodation considerations dictated their move to Chhapara in 1951. Some of the older children moved in the early 1940's to attend the mission school in Chhapara. Jaiwanti, Prakash, and Peter Macleod, who himself became a teacher in the school, were already in Chhapara when Nan arrived. Part of her work in Chhapara when she was doing language study was to help with the care of these children. She would sometimes also have a tiny baby in her room at nights.

Rev Prakash MacLeod looks back on those early days: "As I muse on the early years of my life, instantly one figure who affected my life so much comes vividly to my mind. That figure is none other than Miss A J Dunlop, fondly known as *Mamaji*, meaning 'Respected Mother.' And really she was a mother for all the people in Chhapara, which has been her field of work. I remember a day when I was about eight or nine years of age, studying in class four, and living in the Free Church Orphanage in Chhapara, when we were told of the arrival of a white lady. Expectantly and eagerly we waited for her to come and at last I was able to look at her as she appeared at the mission bungalow. My first impression was of a stern and strict type of person, but soon our fears were removed when we found her to be cheerful, social and loving. It was not long until we realised that we were experiencing motherly love."

Mrs Gajaribai Lall was in charge of the children through the *Toriya* years and her daughter Tarabai, the Biblewoman, who also helped in the hospital dispensary, was their teacher. She was a qualified nursery teacher and took the children through to their state examinations after Primary 4, doing a very good job. She also sewed for the children and made them clothes. After the Chhapara Middle School closed in 1940 due to a shortage of qualified staff, the mission children went to Boarding Schools run by other Missionary Societies, in Jabalpur and other places.

### A Notable Conversion

Munshiram Tiwari was a Brahman priest who was converted under Murray Macleod's ministry in 1943, about a year before Nan arrived. He maintained his faith in Christ from the beginning, but was unwilling to begin his new life as a Christian, after baptism, in his home village of Lakhnadon. He wanted to move to another area. Murray Macleod saw both sides of the problem: "It is easy for us to underestimate the price he must pay if he becomes an open believer here in Lakhnadon. As a Brahman priest he has been used all his life to adulation that amounts even to worship. Now in place of that, he must be willing (quite literally) to become as the off-scouring of all things, exposed to the contempt of those who previously vied for his favour." But more importantly: "The value of his witness for our tiny struggling cause, would be, potentially, very great—if that witness be given locally. Otherwise, it might well prove to be of little or no value so far as encouraging others is concerned. It should also be added that a fearless local witness would effectively shut the mouths of those scorners, who, in their pride, scoffingly say (and in their hearts really believe) that no Brahman could ever become a Christian. But should he begin his Christian life elsewhere, they—while sorely nonplussed—would still be able to say, 'He dared not face us after doing so.'"

Murray Macleod delayed Tiwari's baptism for two years trying to resolve the problem, but finally he did baptise him and his wife in 1945, after they had moved out from Lakhnadon village to the *Toriya*. Tiwari made a vow at that time that he would never cross the river between the *Toriya* and Lakhnadon again unless he turned back to the Hindu faith—and he never did. Dr Donald MacDonald, who went to Lakhnadon as a medical missionary in 1973, recalls an account of the circumstances of Tiwari's vow, later given to him: "As he was leaving the village and crossing the bridge going towards the *Toriya*, he was being taunted by the people that he would soon be returning over the bridge as a Hindu. There and then he made the vow that he would never cross the bridge again unless as a Hindu." When Tiwari went down to Seoni to leave his eldest boy there in Boarding School, many Brahmans followed him on the bus and on cycles. In a debate with them, Tiwari said: "If a diamond were lying on the ground and a man ignorant of its value trampled it underfoot, the diamond would think nothing of that, but if a jeweller came and recognised it to be genuine, yet trampled it underfoot, the diamond would be greatly offended because the jeweller who recognised its value did this. Well, I'm the jeweller. I know the value of Jesus as Saviour—so how could I trample the diamond underfoot?"

## The Move to Chhapara

After lengthy consideration, Murray Macleod found himself at variance with the church on the subject of infant baptism, and when he and the family left for home-leave in November 1945, it was all but certain that they would not return. Nan had now become involved in every part of the work in Chhapara, and felt that the Lord had laid it on her heart to move there. When she made the offer to Murray Macleod he replied that he and his wife had been praying for this, but that they had not wanted to ask her directly. To them it was a direct and wonderful answer to prayer. So Nan moved to Chhapara eleven months after her arrival in India. She was the only missionary there and Dr Annie the only missionary in Lakhnadon. When he was leaving, Murray Macleod handed Nan over to Charan Masih, the mission cook at Chhapara, who was extremely good to her. If she went out at night without telling him, for example, he would soon be out with the lantern looking for her. She profited much from his wise counsel for twenty years. Tiwari and his family had already moved to Chhapara where he worked as an Evangelist and as a part-time teacher in the school. He had considerable intellectual and speaking gifts but was greatly in need of Christian teaching. He and Murray Macleod had great mutual respect, and the missionary's homegoing was a hard knock for Tiwari.

However, Nan gained Tiwari's confidence and developed a strong relationship with him and his family. Mrs Sarah Macleod, looking back in 1996, provides this graphic insight: "Nan was of special help to us during these years in connection with the many adjustments that Tiwari and his wife had to make. She was aware of the complications they faced as they settled into an entirely new way of life. Tiwari's father, who was a well-to-do government official, had promised to support him financially when he became the leading Brahman priest in the area. In this role he was accustomed to people of all castes (up to the highest) falling prostrate before him with their foreheads on his feet. After his conversion he simply walked away from all that, taking with him only a few necessities, leaving a huge home and losing not just his income but the prospect of a share in his father's will. To his family and friends he had become an outcast. Not all members of the mission community fully understood his situation, but Nan was always most supportive. Tiwari and his wife were keenly appreciative of the sensitive and outgoing way in which she helped them settle in."

We will meet Tiwari again in the next chapter, as we see Nan emerging from a severe and unexpected crisis.

# 6

# Crisis and Recovery

In December 1946, just two years after her arrival, Nan was back on board ship in Bombay. She was en route to the UK accompanying another missionary who was sick and returning home to Scotland. She had her trunk with her, the one she went out with, packed with all her belongings. She had said nothing to Dr Annie or to anyone else about her true state of mind, but on looking back on the occasion and its circumstances, Nan believes that she would not have returned to India. We have had no hint of trouble in the first year, so what happened or developed during the second to make her feel she could not continue? As the story unfolds we will see that it was not one thing, but the cumulative effect of several things that was responsible. A multiplicity of problems can make us think that just too much is wrong.

## The Growing Crisis

One of the factors in the developing situation was tension between Tiwari and the small local church. There were just fourteen in the Chhapara church at that time, including five children. We would expect that the Christians would be delighted that a person of such prominence had been converted and had joined them. But they did not accept him very well at first. Perhaps they had a grievance over his unwillingness to take his stand in Lakhnadon. Perhaps there were some who feared that the arrival of a dominant figure would change the status quo to their disadvantage. Tiwari, for his part, was a proud and forceful man, like the Brahmans as a whole, who were the highest Hindu caste. It would show in the way he would ask people to do things. He did not always display humility of spirit and he had not yet learned to guard his tongue or manage his temper properly. Nan remembers a visit to his family on one occasion. They did not eat meat themselves but Tiwari made his wife kill a chicken to cook for Nan. She confided in Nan afterwards that she had to pray before she killed it because she did not know how she could go through with it. Nan explained, "*No-one could have told Tiwari 'No.'*" The situation gave rise to problems and there was a round of mutual complaining. Tiwari's house was stoned and he believed it was Christian boys who were responsible. They certainly gave him a derogatory name.

This, of course, is a picture of Tiwari at the very beginning of his growth in grace, with no Christian background or influence at all, and as yet possessing very, very little Biblical knowledge. His gifts, grace, and potential were never in doubt to those who knew him well, and Rev Duncan Leitch, visiting the Indian field in 1955 on behalf of the Foreign Missions Committee paid him this tribute: "Mr Tiwari is, in my opinion, the ablest of our evangelists... . I believe him to be a truly born-again man who, in the face of many difficulties and not a little opposition, has been faithful to the Lord, for whom he has a deep love." Nan got on well with him and felt a special burden for him. With John McNeel's help she organised the building of a house for him, joined to the side of the school, just across the road from the mission house where she lived. That was a considerable task for

Nan and was part of the pressure at the beginning of the second year. But Tiwari and his wife, Mahangibai, were unfailingly good to Nan and they enjoyed a cordial relationship. Tiwari, himself, was always gracious. Nan remembers Mahangibai sitting in her house cleaning the grain, with her Bible beside her, learning what she could as she worked. Tiwari's contribution to the work of the Kingdom was to be considerable, but there were those integration difficulties in Chhapara at the beginning. Nan found it all a constant strain.

Another factor was the acute political and religious antagonism that year. The campaign for Indian independence, of which Nan had had her first experience when she docked at Bombay in December 1944, gained momentum, complicated and passionately embittered by the conflict between Hindus and Muslims. Early in 1946 the British government offered independence to India. But the Indian National Congress, which was predominantly Hindu, and the Muslim League, could not agree. The Muslim League escalated the tension in declaring 16 August 1946 an Action Day to achieve the setting up of Pakistan as a separate Muslim nation. Violence and bloodshed between Hindus and Muslims erupted in Calcutta the next day, and before long spread to many parts of India. In the following year British and Indian leaders agreed to partition India as the only way to put an end to the Hindu-Muslim violence. Consequently, India became an independent dominion in the British Commonwealth on 15 August 1947, and Pakistan, the day before. But the changes failed to stop the widespread bloodshed and sometimes whole village populations were slaughtered in the conflict.

Even in Chhapara, in 1946, there were people shouting in the streets to put the English out. They painted anti-British slogans on the walls. Some of them urged a boycott of the English language. At that time there was no bank in Seoni and Nan had to go to Jabalpur for any financial transactions. On one of her visits the bank teller said to her: "The manager would like to see you." No-one likes to be summoned by a bank manager, and Nan was a little apprehensive as she went to his office. But he only said: "I just wanted to see the woman who lives in that village alone, for I get in and out of it as quickly as I can with my life!" He was a Scotsman, and went to Chhapara to assess collateral offered as security for his bank loans. Traders often sought loans to fund the hemp fibre trade which flourished in Chhapara at that time.

Tension grew between Muslims and Hindus too, which spilled over into violence in the village towards the end of 1947. By contrast there was much that was pleasant and neighbourly. The people showed Nan real kindness and greatly appreciated her work among them. Nan, for her part, had adjusted well to their culture and way of life. She recalls her walks to the dispensary in the goldsmiths' quarter at the other end of the village from the mission house where she lived. Her route took her through two or three *mohallas*, and some Brahman children used to run and meet her as she passed along. One day a little fellow put his arms around her legs, hidden by her *sari*, and then said, "Ah, your feet are white!" The children had never noticed any difference. So it would be quite wrong to think that community tension or anti-British feeling dominated the local scene. But the sentiments that were expressed proved a daily strain, and rebuffed Nan's open spirit of identity.

Then there was the very moving case of Darla Mackenzie. Darla was from Ross-shire in Scotland and arrived in India early in 1946 as a Biblewoman. She was a lovely person, but her short stay in India, as it turned out to be, was a time of difficulty and considerable distress for her. She suffered greatly from the heat as temperatures soared towards 110° in the early summer. At the end of April she went north with Nan to Landour in the hills for language study, but found progress difficult. She became unwell there and was unable to return to the plains until the end of July, somewhat after the scheduled time. Nan stayed with her. But Darla's greatest trial was the extreme poverty. She could not bear the thin, undernourished children and the skinny animals. By the end of the year it was agreed that Darla should return home, and Nan, to whom she had attached herself with great dependence, was asked to accompany her to Scotland. Perhaps home looked suddenly very attractive to Nan too, as she dismantled her work and prepared to leave. But undoubtedly the sequence had affected her very deeply.

Without a doubt there were other underlying factors which contributed to Nan's year of growing crisis. These may have been more powerful than the issues we have described, and it may be too that Nan was not specifically conscious of them. The newness of the first year, with all its initial stimulus and excitement was over. There was the loss of Murray Macleod with his qualities of leadership and high reputation with which the mission identified. If there was any question about it being a "tiny struggling cause" before, there could be little doubt now. Nan remained the sole missionary in Chhapara, just 28 years old, and only in her second year. For a missionary at the very beginning of her career the effects of loneliness and tiredness, along with the pressures of responsibility and decision-making, may also have been at work. In addition, she had responsibility for the school, and there were particular difficulties in that year. The Foreign Missions Committee, to their great credit, were acutely aware of these dangers and doing everything in their power to resource the work. But response was slow. And the church at home may have failed to some degree too. Perhaps there was lack of prayer, a waning of interest and correspondence, all noticeable to the missionary, and effectively contributing to a feeling of isolation. Above all, Nan "wrestled not against flesh and blood, but against principalities, against powers, against the rulers of the darkness of this world." (Eph 6:12)

## The Turning Point

At Bombay Nan and Darla met some people who were travelling home to Britain, and in a short time they knew one another well enough to explain the reason for their journey. These friends took an immediate interest in the situation and urged Nan not to leave Dr Mackay alone, assuring her that they would escort Darla safely home. Nan thought of Dr Annie and weighed it up. "The 'Quit India' movement is in full swing," she debated with herself, "but the British Embassy will send someone regularly to check that all is well." This was the turning point for Nan, and she resolved to go back. The Embassy visits were nothing like enough to ease her mind. And revealing something of the pain and conflict going on within her as she waved good-bye to Darla, she recalled this vivid memory: "She was standing up there on that ship and her face was white, terribly white. She just looked so very, very sick."

Nan left Bombay and caught the train back to Jabalpur, where she slept in the station overnight. It was Christmas Eve, 1946. Next morning she paid a visit to the station shop which enables us to conclude this difficult and memorable year on a lighter note. Knowing nothing of the Free Church of Scotland practice of celebrating New Year, but not Christmas, she bought from the shop a supply of balloons and Christmas decorations for the children, and decorated the place for them as soon as she got back! "Dr Annie didn't say anything," Nan observed with an air of summing up. "She was very good. And that was the start of Christmas!" Nan's departure with Darla, under the circumstances, had obviously been a fairly quiet affair, so her short absence passed unnoticed by many. The few who assumed she was now on the high seas, and away for several months, were truly taken by surprise—and delighted! Darla arrived home safely and made a good recovery. She was well enough to visit Belfast early in 1947 and for more than 30 years she generated interest and prayer for India from her home in the north of Scotland.

It is a matter for particular thankfulness that the turning point for Nan came before she left the shores of India, and that God "who giveth more grace" gave her that all important triumph. But would she have returned to India had she continued home to Belfast in 1946? Yes—in spite of the doubts that still remain. Rest, prayer, reflection, the need of the people and the children she had left, and above all, her living missionary call would have brought her to Chhapara again. And that question, raised once by Rev W J Grier, about "putting the hand to the plough and looking back" could have returned to the agenda too—and this time with no dispute! Nan wrote to her church on 24 November 1948: "I want you to pray that I may be faithful in presenting the Lord Jesus to these poor ignorant folks. It's not easy to speak for Him at home and it is even more difficult to witness for Him out here. Please pray that the Lord will keep me faithful." This was the same person who in 1946 was leaving, with the thought she would never return. She was then in the trial of discouragement, but two years later she is recovered, strengthened in perseverance through her hard experience.

**Encouragement**

Much needed, much prayed-for encouragement came for everyone early in 1947. It had looked entirely otherwise with only Dr Annie and Nan remaining, and Dr Annie due to go on furlough in the middle of the year. But Miss Elizabeth Macleod who had retired in 1944, shortly before Nan arrived, came out of retirement and sailed for India in March. Rev Duncan Leitch described her offer to go back at such a time of need as "an act of devotion and self-denial that has stirred the whole church." She stayed for eighteen months, working mostly in Lakhnadon. The Elizabeth Macleod Memorial Reading Room was opened in 1964 between the mission house and the school in Chhapara's Christian *'mohalla.'* A new missionary, Miss Janette Brown from Edinburgh, later Mrs Gailey, arrived at the same time as Miss Elizabeth to begin a twelve-year span of service. She too was a nurse, with particular experience as a Health Visitor. She spent her first three years in Lakhnadon and then moved to Chhapara for the rest of her career. She recalls how she and Nan sang psalms and hymns together in the evenings, achieving a measure of success with two-part harmony.

The orphans used to join with them too, especially after church on Sunday evenings.

But the encouragement was not unbroken, for when Nan was in the hills at Landour, in May of that year, 1947, she received a cable informing her of the death of her brother-in-law, her sister Mary's husband, in a motor-cycle accident. It happened just three weeks after the birth of their son. It was Nan's first experience of family grief since coming to India, and she felt her sister's loss very deeply.

It was a boost for everyone when news came through that Murray and Sarah Macleod would after all be returning with their family at the end of August. They were happy to serve the mission for two more years, before entering their planned new sphere of service. It was a personal privilege and pleasure for Nan to know that her former colleagues would be coming back, if only temporarily, and she wrote with expectation: "We are looking forward with joy to the return of the Macleod family. We hope that Mr Macleod will have some special meetings for the upbuilding of the Christians here." God was soon to reward that hope in quite a memorable way. The work in India was never well resourced numerically with missionary staff, but we thank God that, apart from times of furlough, it was not until 1985-88, when government restrictions were bringing missionary activity to a close, that missionary numbers were as low as they were in 1946.

There was encouragement among the children too. Nan wrote at the end of 1946: "The children here learn the Shorter Catechism. Prakash has got as far as the 102nd answer. He is greatly excited about it. Daya, Tiwari's youngest boy, has reached answer 35. He wants to learn it all so that he also will win an English Bible. The other three children are smaller than Daya and Prakash, but they are doing quite well. They take worship by turns every night and always remember the people in Ireland and Scotland. It thrills me to hear them singing the praises of the Lord in this dark place."

### Lakhnadon Again and a New Bicycle

When Dr Annie went home on furlough in the middle of 1947, Nan moved up to Lakhnadon to take charge of the hospital. The monsoons were delayed that year, there was an outbreak of cholera in the Central Provinces, and there were other difficulties too which made her conscious of her dependence on the Lord: "The heat is very trying just now. Four of the orphan children in our care have had bad attacks of dysentery and most of them have had some eye trouble; so we are fairly busy with them. I feel most inadequate for the work at the hospital, but the Lord never fails." Among those orphans would have been the twins, Samuel and Daniel Masih, who arrived at that time when they were seven months old. Tarabai accepted them from their mother when the missionaries were out and from that day became mother to them.

*The Irish Evangelical* of September 1947 reported that the United Young People's Meeting (Botanic Avenue and Lisburn Road Churches) had collected money for the purchase of a bicycle for Nurse Dunlop. It also quoted from one of Nan's letters: "I do very much want a bicycle. It was lovely of the Young People's Meeting to think of it. I am delighted at the prospect of having a bicycle of my own." The December edition recorded her enthusiastic appreciation of the gift, expressed in the context of her maternity calls: "It has been a great boon for I have been called out fairly often lately and mostly in a hurry. Maternity cases have been plentiful, and I would like you to pray for wisdom and skill for me, as most of the cases to which I am called really are cases which require a doctor and things crop up which I would never have to face at home."

Nearly 50 years later one memory of the bicycle stands out: "I came off that bicycle with such an awful bang that I didn't use it again! I was coming down the *Toriya* hill—and the *chakra* was going down ahead of me. The driver was near the bottom of the hill—and if he had gone on... . But he stopped the thing when he saw me. He must have stopped it to let me past—but it wasn't to let me past, for there was no room and I had to swerve to the side. I think I hit a stone! The handlebar went into me, and oh dear, it was terrible!" However, the bicycle continued in use, fulfilling its commission in other hands.

## Independent India and the Gospel

We have already noted the significance of 1947 for India, with national independence finally being gained in that year. But independence soon began to have consequences for missions. Almost immediately the new government introduced legislation to tackle the issue of religious conversion. The Public Safety Act in Madhya Pradesh contained an Anti-Conversion Clause which required any person wanting to change his religion to appear alone before a magistrate, to satisfy him of sincerity and of freedom from inducement. This gave the magistrates, often resolutely opposed to Christianity, considerable influence. And the formal legal procedures were intimidating, in themselves, for any who would espouse the Christian faith and declare their new life in public baptism. Murray Macleod had difficulty in assessing the extent to which the new Act would apply in the Central Provinces. At first it appeared that it would affect only specified districts where there were Muslim concentrations of population. And so there was early thankfulness that the new converts of the mission area would be spared the ordeal of appearing before a magistrate. It was even reported before the end of 1948 that the government had revoked the Anti-Conversion Clause. But such relief was premature for it soon became apparent that laws to monitor conversion to Christianity would continue. And they have to the present time.

Nan recalled a case which was affected by the general mood of the new arrangements. Sometime during the monsoon season, July-September, in 1947 or 1948, when she was in Lakhnadon covering for Dr Annie, a man arrived with a new baby. His wife had died. He was from one of the outlying villages and had been carrying the baby on his head for miles through the rain. In the circumstances of the new legislation Nan had no option but to send him on to the police station in Lakhnadon to obtain permission for her to take the baby. This was a walk of nearly half an hour. The police in turn sent the man to the magistrate who sent him back again to the police. He finally returned to the *Toriya*, with authorisation for the mission to treat the baby, but not to keep it. The next day two local government officials came to see Nan, and said: "Remember, you're not allowed to keep that baby." Nan replied, "Yes, I know I'm not allowed to keep it. And I don't think you're going to keep it either. I think that baby is going to go to God! Just you come and see it." The baby had pneumonia and in fact died within a short time.

Communal disturbances continued after partition and independence, and they sometimes had an underlying effect on the work. Towards the end of 1947, just months after Independence Day, Murray Macleod described the incident we earlier mentioned in passing: "We have had an outbreak of Hindu-Moslem rioting here in Chhapara. The Muslims had killed a cow (the animal worshipped and revered by Hindus); a Hindu remonstrated and was struck. In a short time the village was in an uproar and a fierce fight broke out between the two groups. The Muslims, being heavily outnumbered, had to flee to the jungles and many have not yet ventured to return to their homes but are living in groups in nearby villages which have Muslim landlords. A large contingent of police arrived from Seoni and quickly restored order." However, the Lakhnadon-Chhapara area was spared the excesses of other districts and generally remained quiet.

Against this background of legislation and potential party strife the mission had freedom to work and evangelise. But opposition was not only from the Hindu and Muslim religions. A large number of Roman Catholic priests and nuns, both European and Indian, travelled to India with Nan on the same ship, and one of Nan's frequent worries in these early years was the advancement of the Roman Catholic Church in the villages of their area. Yet there were many opportunities. The five children of the Chhapara congregation came to the mission bungalow every evening for worship. Although very young, and at first reluctant, they took turns at reading the Bible portion and praying. The Biblewoman concluded with prayer after them. On Tuesday afternoons the women held a prayer meeting at the bungalow and included in their prayer agenda were the home churches of the missionaries! By the beginning of 1949 there were 140 children in the Chhapara

*Tiwari, Dr. Annie, Murray &
Sarah Macleod, Nan, Alister and
Morrison Macleod in the 1940s*

*Landour, 1945*

*Chhapara Sunday School in the late 1940s*

*Rev. George Sutherland,*
*Mary MacDonald,*
*Dr. Jeannie Grant,*
*Rev. John McNeel,*
*Mary McNeel,*
*Babs Sutherland, Nan*
*and Sutherland children*

*Vilmala, Nan, Mervyn Oliver,*
*Kamala - Early 1960's*

*Mrs Ruthbai Salve, Nan, Miss Tarabai Lal, Mr. Patail, Contractor,*
*Ian McKenzie, Tiwari, visitor, Mr. Shastri, Evangelist,*
*Dr. Annie Mackay, Heather Beaton (foreground)*
*Laying the foundation stone for new staff bungalow, 1966*

*Mrs Elizabeth Macleod, Tarabai Lall, Nan,*
*Rev. Samuel Washington, Shantibai, Rahibai,*
*Dr. Annie with children, 1947*

*Janette Brown*

*Rev. & Mrs. Pakash Kumar and*
*family c. 1995*

*Bringing the Ambulance from Bombay with*
*Heather Beaton and John Farley, 1966*

Kashmir

Pakistan

Nepal

Delhi ▪

Landour ●

Mussoorie

● Kachwa

Allahabad ●

● Varanasi

Pachmarthi ●

● Jabalpur

● Bihar

Parasia ●

Chhindwara ●

● Seoni

Padhar ●

● Rukhvar

● Nagpur

● Bombay

Mission Area
See opposite

Madras ●

● Ootacamund

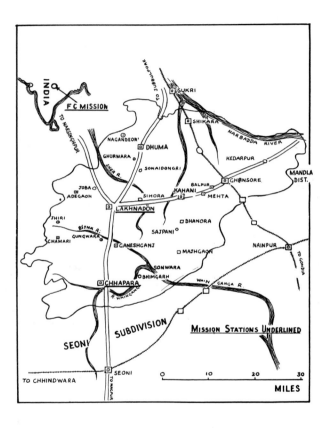

*Location map*

*A page from Dr. Annie Mackay's village visitation record*

*Mary Ann MacDonald*

*Dr. Helen Ramsay*

*Dr. Anne Urquhart*

*Flora Macleod*

*Heather Beaton*

Lady Missionaries 1970 (Courtesy *Labourers Together*)

*On a vist to India 1982*

*Nan and Heather Beaton on a visit to India 1988*

*Miss M. K. Speers, Mr. J.D.P Blair, Mrs Isabella Dunlop, Mrs Wilkinson, 1967*

*With Alexander John in Belfast, June 1995*

Sunday School, nearly all of them Hindus or Muslims. Up in Lakhnadon, Janette Brown started a playhour twice a week with books, 'snakes and ladders' and a box of Macleod family toys. The children loved it and even the bigger ones came in after school. In the summer of 1948 Nan added a children's meeting on Tuesday afternoons, holding it on the verandah just outside her own room. There were 24 names on the roll.

Turning to the work at the dispensary, Nan was kept busy during her year at Lakhnadon. She described an interesting cultural scene in April 1948: "The grain harvest is finished, so the women have time to come and have treatment for their aches and pains. It's the women here who cut the grain. They do it with sickles. It's an awful job, and I don't wonder that they come in flocks wanting oil for rubbing." Often she asked for prayer for the evangelistic side of the medical work: "I need your prayers that 'utterance may be given unto me that I may open my mouth boldly to make known the mystery of the Gospel.' It is often very hard to introduce the message, patients are so interested in themselves and in the medicine, and the devil does his best to keep one's mouth shut." She returned to Chhapara in October 1948 when Dr Annie resumed at Lakhnadon, and immediately started having around 50 patients a day at the re-opened dispensary, soon going up to 80. She wrote in similar vein: "It's not easy work. The children cry, and the women talk about different things while Rahilbai, the Biblewoman, is speaking." Just at that time she was called out to a girl of about twelve who was ill with fever, probably malaria. She was delirious and the family were sure that she was going to die. One of the men said to another, "Go on, put the evil spirit out of her." Nan said, "If you are going to do things like that I will leave!" The man did nothing and Nan prayed a simple prayer. She gave the girl some aspirin in hot water, the only medication she had with her, and left another with a long list of instructions. The girl recovered.

The work of evangelistic camps went on as well. At one camp early in 1947 Nan and Gajaribai, who looked after the *Toriya* orphans, treated 521 patients and visited 30 of the surrounding villages. Nan did not go to camp in 1948, but instead went with Gajaribai's daughter Tarabai on a series of village visits on Tuesdays and Thursdays. They presented a message and then dispensed the medicines. Nan wrote of these visits: "Do remember us in this work. The people are very backward and often do not understand much of what is being said. Truly the god of this world has blinded their minds. Would God the light of the glorious Gospel would shine in and dispel the darkness!"

## Known by Name

The work in India never experienced rapid growth or significant numbers of new converts, although on a few occasions whole villages were strongly influenced by the Gospel. The story so often focuses on the lives of individuals. One of these from the earlier years was Tiwari to whose story we now return. After the departure of Murray Macleod Nan frequently mourned the lack of systematic teaching for Tiwari, and of a man to do it. It was clear from Tiwari's messages and prayers that he was making real progress but of course he made mistakes. He prayed for rain one day in the spring of 1946, and it rained so heavily that night that the water poured through the roof on to his bed when he was asleep! The amazing speed and effectiveness of the answer frightened him but greatly strengthened his faith. He then urged people to pray to his God for rain whenever they needed it and He would surely send it! In February 1947 Nan urged more prayer for Tiwari. His only brother shot himself because Tiwari would not respond to his pleadings and return to Hinduism. Food was also scarce at that time and because of his Christian stand Tiwari found it difficult to obtain his rations. Nan described him as 'troubled on every hand.' He became anxious too for the conversion of his eldest son Jyotish, at High School in Seoni, and under intense pressure from Hindus, especially his relatives. Tiwari requested prayer for him, and not long after the Lord strengthened his faith still more by His answer.

In 1948, Murray Macleod, back in Chhapara, described Tiwari as "wonderfully growing both in knowledge and grace." That year he took him and Godwin Laxman, the man who gave Nan her first lessons in Hindi at the village camp, to Allahabad for special classes for lay preachers. Around this time correspondence noted that Tiwari's eyes were ready for cataract operation. This was such good news because he longed to get back to reading the Hindi Old Testament; only the New was available in large type, and even that he could read with only one eye. Tiwari began to ask for prayer also for his younger son Daya, a rather wild lad, who had gone to Seoni Mission High School to join his brother Jyotish. We noted earlier that he was one of the young people learning the Shorter Catechism. Nan said, with prophetic insight: "I do not know what will become of him if he does not soon give his heart to the Lord." Later that year, Daya, then only sixteen, ran away from home for the fifth time.

Foremost among the mission names were the orphans, and the most memorable evangelistic event of the period was a movement of the Spirit among them at the beginning of 1948. It was during special New Year and Communion services. The meetings began on Sunday 28 December and concluded eight days later with a thanksgiving service on the Monday, after the communion of the previous day. During the week they held meetings at 8.15 am and at 4.15 pm with an afternoon children's tent meeting on Monday, Tuesday and Wednesday. Murray Macleod was the preacher. The primary purpose of the meetings was the upbuilding of believers, for which Nan had expressed an expectant desire when she heard of the Macleods' return. No doubt the believers were strengthened, but the great outcome of the meetings was that six of the orphans and Tiwari's eldest son, Jyotish, either professed faith in Christ or became seriously concerned about the issues of salvation. These orphans were Prakash, Peter Macleod, Shushila (later Peter's sister-in-law), Taramoni and her brother Yunas, and Jaiwanti. Taramoni and Shushila were school boarders at Jabalpur at the time, and the other four children were at Lakhnadon, although Prakash and Yunas also went to Boarding School at Jabalpur three months later. Nan spent some time with these young people in the mornings before going down to the hospital, and read to them from Frances Ridley Havergal's book of daily readings, 'Morning Bells.' A few years passed before some of them came to true personal faith, but a memorable work of God was done at that time.

Included also in the names of those who became familiar to missionary readers were some who gave promising and extended responses to the Gospel but did not finally make a definite Christian commitment.

Jharu was one such person. He was from Chhapara and professed faith through contact with Tiwari during Nan's first term. In 1946 and again in 1951, on Nan's return from furlough, he asked her for baptism, but Nan felt they should wait until his Christian stand was clearer. Nan hoped that his wife would also become a Christian. At first Mrs Jharu had bitterly opposed her husband's stand, and they had separated, but she began to show some interest and came to see him several times. They had two young children. Jharu was staying in the mission compound at Chhapara and some men, who said that Nan had locked him up, threatened her with a stick. They were all shouting at once and at that stage she was unable to follow all of their excited clamour. They told her, among other things, that no-one would ever allow her into their home again. She took them to see Jharu at the compound, but he refused to go outside the gate. He gave them his testimony from inside it.

During this period Jharu was making good progress, bright and anxious to learn. Often as he came to worship in the mornings he could be heard learning a verse of a Psalm or an answer from the Catechism, as he walked. A year on, however, Jharu suddenly broke with Christian friends and persistently avoided all efforts to contact him. Nan saw him from time to time during the next year without having an opportunity to speak with him, but six months before her first furlough she did have contact with his wife through providing medical attention for her and one of the children. She was able to visit his wife again and spoke to Jharu's brother and some other women who had gathered.

Another name from Nan's first term with whom we must become acquainted is David—David Talib

Masih, born in 1948. He was given into Nan's care at Lakhnadon when he was just an infant, during the time Dr Annie was away, and Nan took him back to Chhapara with her on Dr Annie's return. David did not turn out well and Nan continues to feel a measure of responsibility for that. He became very attached to her in those early months of his life, looking to her as a child would to its own mother. Of course there were times of separation as Nan travelled around and went off on holiday, and also during an epidemic of plague and typhoid in Chhapara, when David was transferred to Lakhnadon. When Nan came home on furlough in December 1949 she left him in the orphanage which by then had effectively moved to Chhapara. But Nan was never able to recover that early relationship with David and she still feels that that break played a significant part in his future.

## Concluding the First Term

About three months before she left on furlough in early December 1949, Nan was ill and off duty for three weeks. Although it was the rainy season, she walked through Chhapara to the dispensary with nothing on her feet but flip-flops. It was muddy and dirty, and so bad in places that one day the sole of one of the flip-flops stuck fast in the mud and stayed behind, leaving Nan with just the upper. Later in the day she stood up from where she was writing prescriptions and immediately knew something was wrong. "Oh dear," she said, "I don't know what's happened to me!" Rahilbai, the Biblewoman who was dispensing the medicines said, "I can tell you what's happened. There's a red line running up the back of your leg. It's poison!" Nan must have had a graze or break on her heel as she walked through the mud and dirt and picked up a virulent infection.

She got home with considerable difficulty and immediately went across to Tiwari's house. She was so weak by this time that it took both Tiwari and his wife to help her back home. Tiwari had some experience with Ayurvedic medicine, the ancient system of medicine based on the Hindu Vedic scriptures, and assessing the seriousness of the condition, he sent by bus to Lakhnadon for Dr Annie, who came immediately, arriving at Chhapara the next morning. Nan suffered severe pain during that first night. Mahangibai, Tiwari's wife, sat up with her throughout it and continued to do so for several nights, reading especially from the Psalms and praying. Dr Annie had taught her to read. Evidently she had been reading from Revelation 12 about the serpent, for which the Hindi Bible uses the word 'python'—the large snake which crushes and swallows its prey. Mahangibai prayed: "Lord, that old serpent the devil—he tries to swallow everybody like a python. He's trying to swallow her up Lord and don't you let him do that. Lord, you did that for Job." Dr Annie stayed with Nan for five days, treating her 4-hourly with crystalline penicillin injections. She responded to the treatment, and to Dr Annie's devoted, exclusive care, and recovered. But Nan has retained a conviction through the years that Mahangibai's prayer on the critical first night was that of one of the righteous—effectual and availing much.

Nan sailed from Bombay on her first furlough on 9 December on SS Corfu, and once again the journey was far from uneventful. As she was passing through the Red Sea she became ill with heart trouble. The ship's doctor confined her to bed and prescribed sublingual tablets. Another doctor on board, a missionary to Manchuria, said to Nan afterwards, "I thought you were going to die." Nan said, "I did too!" Another doctor she met on board advised her never to go back and live alone again... ."Which I promptly did after I went back." Another passenger she met urged her to settle down at home and not to go back 'to that place.' "They put a bomb under my bed in Calcutta," he said... . "But," Nan said, "I went!"

Nan's Welcome Home was held in her own church on 19 January 1950. Rev W J Grier was unable to attend because of illness but sent a letter of greeting. Rev C E Hunter presided in his absence. Miss M K Speers, a former Sunday School teacher of Nan's recalled Nan's keenness during her Sunday School days. Nan's good friend, Margaret Williamson took part as soloist. Rev W J McDowell in welcoming Nan on behalf of the whole church, exhorted everyone present to concentrate on supporting the church's own missionaries. Nan, after bringing formal greetings from the church in India, thanked all who had remembered her work in prayer. She explained that the work in India was surrounded with obstacles peculiar to that land. She told of those who were kept from coming out openly for Christ because of the caste system, which curtailed individual freedom in a way altogether unknown at home. She requested, as she was to do on future occasions, intercession for more missionaries, reminding the congregation that while she was at home, Dr Annie Mackay and Miss Janette Brown would be the only European workers in the field with its 800 villages. The proceedings ended with the singing of Psalm 72:17-19, and prayer by Rev C H Garland.

What were Nan's thoughts about what she had accomplished in the five years? "I don't think I accomplished very much," she said. The question was not a good one, but the answer was hopelessly inadequate. It overlooked so much. For the mission had achieved a Christian influence far out of proportion to its size and resources. Thousands had received the love and practical benefit of medical attention in the name of Christ, and the foundation was laid for far better things to come. Children had been given Christian education, orphans taken into care. Through village camps, dispensaries, hospital, and visits to homes, thousands of patients and relatives had heard the Gospel. In Sunday Schools and Children's Meetings the Good News was presented to many children. There was the blessing among the orphans. There were the individuals, though few, who had responded and grown. Of course it was a 'tiny struggling cause' in terms of missionary numbers and local churches, but there is another perspective: "Now thanks be unto God, which always causeth us to triumph in Christ, and maketh manifest the savour of his knowledge by us in every place. For we are unto God a sweet savour of Christ, in them that are saved, and in them that perish" (2 Cor 2:15). But would missionary opportunity in India continue? This question began to cast a foreboding shadow on the future of the work.

# 7

## "The Night Cometh"

Among the greetings presented to Nan at her valedictory service in her home church at Belfast on 25
January 1951, was one from the missionary staff in
India assuring her of a warm welcome back. The
sender was Rev George Sutherland, the new mission
Superintendent who had arrived with his wife Babs
and their two children in 1950, while Nan was at
home. They served the mission throughout the
1950's. And Nan was accompanied by another new
missionary when she returned in February—Miss
Mary Ann MacDonald, a nurse from the island of
Lewis. In the Bay of Biscay they ran into a severe
storm which raged for five days and they had to
stand by a ship in distress. It was not until they
passed through the Straits of Gibraltar that they entered calmer waters. During the height of the storm
Mary remembered Jonah. She served for twenty
years with a break in the 1960's, and returned for a
brief supplementary spell in 1979. The addition of
these two missionaries in 1950 and 1951 brought
the staff numbers back up to five, the level they had
reached for a short time in the 1930's. There was
always some staff movement between the two cen-
tres, but usually Dr Annie, George Sutherland, and
Mary MacDonald were at Lakhnadon, with Janette
Brown and Nan based at Chhapara.

Nan spent the first few months of her second term at Lakhnadon before taking a short holiday in the hills at Landour, where the new missionaries were at language school. She remembers a lovely little story from that visit involving Mary MacDonald. One of Mary's fellow students there was a Canadian girl called Frances Taylor. One day a local man, whose English was not very good, called at the door, and Mary, who answered, was eventually able to make out 'Fancy Taylor.' "She's not here," Mary said. The man said "Yes, yes," but Mary insisted "No, no"—and limited vocabulary arguments are not necessarily brief. Dr Victor Gardiner, a medical missionary who later became Northern Ireland representative of the Emmanuel Hospital Association was there at the time and heard the dispute. He said to Mary: "He's just trying to tell you that he's a fancy tailor wants your order!"

## Growing Opposition

Before returning to Chhapara in May to begin a new period of service there, Nan went back to Lakhnadon for a month to relieve Dr Annie on holiday, and to be on hand for the older orphans, home from boarding school. The eight younger ones followed her to Chhapara soon after, when the new orphanage was ready. This gave the children ready access to education at the Mission school as well as better accommodation. Godwin Laxman, Nan's old friend from her first camp in December 1944, was now with her in Chhapara, and together they resolved to make a greater effort to bring the people in. They planned the re-commencement of the children's meeting, and a new men's meeting. Nan wrote: "But surely, surely, the Lord has much people in this place—else why did he place us here?" We see the need here for

Nan to encourage herself in the Lord, as she revealed the greatest question in her mind. Response to the Gospel had always been slow, but she had felt a change for the worse since her return. Earlier that year when the hospital was less busy than usual, she had accompanied Dr Annie on a series of village visits by car. Dr Annie would drop her off at a village, drive on to the next herself, and then pick Nan up again on the way back. Nan observed: "As a rule we were well received, though there appears to me to be more active opposition than there was before I went home on furlough; but I think that promises better than indifference. Men have said to the more simple of the village folk, 'Don't buy that book! It's about Jesus Christ. Don't read it!'" In 1952 Nan wrote asking for a special place on the home prayer agenda as they began the winter's work: "We expect opposition which we are experiencing more these days. The people just don't want our Gospel... . When we visited the *melas* or fairs in Lakhnadon and Chhapara during their special new year season— these past few days—we were far from being well received, especially in Chhapara, and we were able to sell very few Gospels." Later she described Lakhnadon as "... an awfully difficult place. It is a stronghold." And she added: "I would rather go anywhere else."

Significantly, government restrictions were increasing too. Correspondence from the middle of 1952 noted that visas were being refused to non-commonwealth missionaries. By 1955 there was news that Commonwealth missionaries would in future be required to apply for visas and that existing missionaries would be wise to obtain a 'No Objection to Return' certificate, before they left on furlough. These regulations became mandatory in 1967. In

1953 a new government Act came into force in Madhya Pradesh, requiring all religious bodies— Hindu, Moslem, and Christian—to register. The next year there was a report that nearly all the people of one village, where another mission was working, had asked for baptism, and that response to evangelism was strong in one or two others. The Indian Evangelist concerned had his work investigated by the police and the villagers had attention from the *Arya Samaj*, an ardent religious Hindu sect, who, as well as running a programme of social work, urged a return to the *Vedas*—the whole body of Hindu scriptures and liturgies. Controversy appeared in the local press over Christian missionaries and alleged forcible conversions. Early in 1955 the Government of the Central Provinces set up the 'Christian Missionary Activities Committee'—George Sutherland attended one of its meetings in Seoni. It reported in 1956. Its wide bibliography included a range of ecclesiastical sources, among them the World Council of Churches. It quoted the well known words of Dr Alexander Duff of Calcutta describing India as "a moral wilderness where all light dies and only death lives underneath one vast catacomb of immortal souls perishing for lack of knowledge," denouncing them as "a vile attack" on the religion of the majority community in India. It accused missionaries in Madhya Pradesh of participation in the 'cold war' and therefore of being a danger to national security. The Committee recommended, among other things, that "Those missionaries whose primary object is proselytization should be asked to withdraw. The large influx of foreign missionaries is undesirable and should be checked." The future for missionary work in the Central Provinces of India looked more uncertain than ever. This was the setting in which Nan and her colleagues evangelised in the 1950's.

## Or Whether They Will Forbear...

Nevertheless the work of evangelism went on in its established way through medical care, camps, distribution of literature at fairs, children's work, village tours, and special winter campaigns in the cooler weather. These winter outreach efforts, for which the missionaries requested prayer and practical help year by year, involved house to house visitation during the day and open-air meetings at night when they sometimes presented a series of special subjects. Nan often displayed a burden of responsibility and a desire that God would work. She said in a letter in January 1952: "Dr Mackay, Rev and Mrs Sutherland and family are out at camp. Miss MacDonald and I hope to join them on Friday. Do pray for us as we go out. So many are dying in sin and ignorance and heathen darkness around us, and great is our responsibility... . We need the prayers of the people at home for a mighty outpouring of the Holy Spirit." Later that year, in October, as they approached the winter's work and its anticipated opposition, she wrote in similar vein: "Pray that we may really be on fire, and as Paul says, that utterance may be given us. We will never be able to carry out our programme except in the strength of the Lord God, and we know and feel it—at least I do, more and more every minute."

Returning to a story from Nan's first year, of the woman from the well-to-do family of silversmiths in Chhapara who came through a time of distress after the birth of one of her children, and afterwards had another baby whom she named 'Indestructible.' This family were very religious—their children worshipped at the family shrine before breakfast in the mornings, even when they were still too young to talk. Nan maintained friendly contact with them and one of them came to her rescue near the beginning of her second term in 1952 during the annual *Dussehra* festival. As part of the celebrations the local Hindu people made a clay image of their feared goddess of destruction, *Durga*, and decked it in pretentious attire. The festival went on for ten days and reached its climax with the crowds marching round the village carrying the goddess on their shoulders before finally throwing it into the river to disintegrate. In preparation for the occasion, the chief men of the village went round the homes and collected subscriptions, and a group of them called on Nan. She made it clear to them that she could not associate in any way with their idol worship, but they were not deterred. They assured her that she had nothing to worry about for no-one would know the source of the donation—it would be attributed simply to 'a very good person.' Nan replied, "My God sees and knows everything."   But the men were insistent, until one of them, a man from this silversmith family, supported Nan's stance and persuaded the others to respect her principles. When the festivities were over, Nan went to see him, "a very fine man and very devout," and read Revelation 21 with him. He promised that he would read the Bible for himself. Later she gave the family a New Testament in the Gujarati language, their mother tongue.

Another religious event at the same time demonstrated the heathen darkness of the field in which the mission worked: "The people here have a 'holy man' buried up to the neck in one of the mud-floors of their houses and grain sown all around him. He is to stay like that for nine days without food or drink.

They water the grain and so the earth is damp. This is the first time this has happened here. They consider him a 'god' of course."

### Glimpses of the Medical Work

The reputation of the mission's medical work increased, and people came from considerable distances, even from as far away as Bombay, especially for maternity care. In January 1952 Nan was able to record: "The people are gaining confidence in us as medicals, especially where maternity work is concerned," but added with deep disappointment, "but there are very few who are concerned to hear what we have to say about their souls." Village calls were an almost daily demand of the medical work. Nan tells of one at the end of a day at the dispensary at Chhapara, itself hard on the heels of a gruelling previous day—and a late night—when the car had stopped ten times on the way to Jabalpur: "A man came to call me to a patient ten miles away, so off we set on horseback. Our journey was in the dark, over rivers, up hills, across mud puddles, and through hemp well above our heads. I could hardly stand on my feet by the time we arrived. We got the patient fixed up and stayed overnight. Godwin was with me, and we spoke to the crowd gathered outside. It was a grand opportunity as there must have been about 100 people present. They listened well, and told us that it was the first time anyone had visited their village."

One night, near the beginning of her second term, Nan was travelling in the car with Rev George Sutherland and his family from Chhapara to Lakhnadon. When they had covered about half the distance, at the village of Ganeshganj, they were stopped by some people who said that a man lying at the side of the road had been murdered. A quick examination revealed that the man had an abdominal knife-wound, extensive and deep enough to leave his intestines protruding. The people had tried to bind him up with an article of clothing, probably a *dhoti*. Severely injured though the man was, Nan knew that he was still alive, so they turned round and rushed him back to Chhapara, to the government hospital there. The doctor could only give the man an injection of morphine but insisted that they take him to the police. Then, after dropping Mrs Sutherland and the children off they drove on south to Seoni— another 21 miles. But their difficulties were really only starting, for it was a festival season and the civil surgeon was not on duty. Only a radiologist was available. He had only seen an operation through a window, he said. He wanted to treat the injured man with saline soaks until the next morning, but Nan was far from sure that he would last the night. When they found an anaesthetist, a lady doctor, Nan persuaded the radiologist to tackle the operation. She scrubbed up to assist, and George Sutherland was the floor-nurse or 'runner', handling utensils and supplying the gallipots with iodine, salve, and spirit. The reluctant 'surgeon' succeeded, including stitching the intestine, and he took a personal post-operative interest in his patient. Antibiotics were scarce, but he canvassed commercial representatives for samples and got what he needed. He wrote to Nan every day, reporting progress, and sent the letters to her at Chhapara by bus. The man recovered. Later, for the Lakhnadon Court, Nan picked the man out in an identity parade by asking the men to lift their shirts.

When Dr Annie was on furlough in 1954, and Nan was covering at Lakhnadon, she tells how her departure for Camp in February was delayed through attending to a bad case of burns: "This poor child's sari caught fire and a considerable part of the upper part of her body was covered with burns. When brought in she was a mass of septic sores, but she is healing now and loves us to pray with her. She was taught John 3:16 when her hair was being done in the mornings and can repeat it almost perfectly. She is nearly fourteen years of age but she cannot read and is not very smart. This morning after I had attended to her, she said: 'After I'm better, I'm not going home. I'm staying here with you. I'll work for you.' Pray for her. I think she has given her heart to the Lord." Sadly, she did not get better, but we have grounds to hope that God, in His strange providence, used her accident and her time in hospital as the means to bring her to grace and not long afterwards to glory. There are other similar cases in the Indian mission story.

Again in 1954, when Dr Annie was away, Nan and Mary MacDonald were doing calls at Kahani, a village about thirteen miles east of Lakhnadon. Tiwari was now living and working there as an evangelist. While they were there they received an urgent call from another village. They agreed that Mary would return to the hospital at Lakhnadon and that Nan would go out to see the patient in the other village, whom she found to be a woman who was very ill. Nan did what she could for her, but by that time it was too late to go home and there was nowhere for her to stay at this village. A policeman then turned up. He was a circuit police supervisor of some kind and he offered Nan accommodation at his house. Nan, assuming all was well, went with him but later found that his wife was not there and the other policemen who were around gradually dispersed. The man gave Nan a room, a little detached from the main house, with a door which could be locked from the outside, but not from the inside! Meanwhile, Tiwari arrived. He had heard about Nan's call-out and had traced her to the policeman's house. Tiwari was cross. He was cross with Nan for finding herself in this position, and cross with the police officer too. He paced up and down outside Nan's room all night and Nan could hear the two men disputing at various times. The next morning Nan's host called her for breakfast. Tiwari said: "She'll eat nothing." The policeman said: "I'll call a bullock-cart then." Tiwari said: "I've called one." Together, these two men escorted Nan to Kahani, riding on bicycles on either side of the bullock-cart, not speaking to each other, each unwilling to yield the right of consort.

Another little anecdote about Mary MacDonald belongs to this time. She was driving by jeep to Nagpur, via Chhindwara on this occasion, with Nan in the passenger seat. Near Chhindwara there were continuous bends for a few miles, sometimes with steep drops on either side, but Mary kept pressing on. Nan was scared but silent. When they were past the bad part, Mary asked: "What did those signs mean which kept saying *Sawadhan*?" "Be Careful!" Nan said tersely. *Sawadhan* was a high Hindi word and Mary at that stage would only have been familiar with the more colloquial *Khabardar*.

## Seconded to Nagpur

1953 became the most notable year of Nan's second term because for nine months of it she was seconded to the Nursing School of the Church of Scotland's Mure Memorial Hospital in Nagpur, the city where Rev Stephen Hislop went as the pioneer missionary in 1844. It was a timely change for Nan in the difficult circumstances of the early 1950's. An emergency had arisen through a lack of nursing tutors and the hospital had requested help which the Foreign Missions Committee were keen for the mission to provide. Nan was a Nursing Superintendent for her time there and a member of the Mid-India Board of Examiners. She said looking ahead to it: "I feel weak and diffident when I think of Nagpur, but I feel it is the right thing. It will, I'm afraid, be one long worry to be responsible for 50 girls there, but the Lord must have some purpose in it. Pray that His purpose may be fulfilled." Dr Annie Mackay, on a furlough visit to Belfast in December 1953, provided the news that Nan had been ill in Nagpur, but that before she was fully recovered, visitors to the Nagpur hospital had reported: "We saw very, very little of her—she was very busy," and, "She is busy as usual." Nan made very good friends at Nagpur, among them, Margaret Ward, whom she still visits in Comrie in Perthshire. She got on very well with the Indian Medical Superintendent, Dr Lucy Augustine, and with Dr Mary Harvie, from Scotland, who sadly fell to her death while hill-walking on holiday in Kashmir some years later.

Nan's illness at Nagpur was tetanus, probably caused by the contamination of a cut knee when she fell coming down the steps at her house, and possibly complicated further by a reaction to the treatment. Tetanus was a very real danger with cows everywhere present. During her stay in hospital she was delirious for a time and at the height of it asked the nurse to straighten the poles of the mosquito net around the bed: "I've been trying to straighten them for the past hour!" she said. A little later she sent for the nurse again, and this time: "Take that dog off the bed!" She recuperated with Margaret Ward and Nan Ross at their home.

Of the interesting stories from the Nagpur months, two concern Tessa, a Roman Catholic Nun from the Republic of Ireland, whom Nan met and used to visit. During the summer of the previous year, when walking home in the dark from a medical call at Chhapara with only a hurricane lamp to light the path, Nan was bitten by a scorpion, and suffered severe pain for a few days. Nan told Tessa about the incident during one of her visits, and the next time she went to see her, Tessa gave her a torch. Referring to her vows of chastity, poverty, and obedience, she said: "I just wish it were better, but you'll understand that it's holy poverty!" When Nan was ill, Tessa came to enquire what was wrong. "Tetanus," Nan replied. "That could kill you," Tessa said, reacting with some alarm, and in a short time Nan had a visit from Father D'Age! He was of The Order of St Francis and was head of the Order's school in Nagpur. Nan found him a pleasant man and good company, and she visited him with Tessa from time to time. They talked about various things including their differing views on proclaiming "The light of the world."

## Rev John McNeel

Another great landmark of Nan's second term was the death of Rev John McNeel of Seoni. It happened as a result of a motor accident in September 1954, when he was 86. The *Irish Evangelical* of November 1954 carried this account based on Nan's correspondence: "Miss Mary McNeel of Seoni had been to Bombay with Nurse Dunlop to meet Dr Annie Mackay. On Dr Mackay's arrival, she and Miss Dunlop agreed to stay over the week-end in Bombay and go to Jabalpur on Monday where Rev George Sutherland was to meet them on Tuesday. Miss McNeel decided to leave immediately (on the Friday, just after Dr Mackay's arrival) for Nagpur. Her father and Rev George Sutherland set out in the car to meet her at Nagpur. Mr Sutherland drove for 40 miles and then Mr McNeel insisted on taking the wheel. It was pouring and there was a tree down across the road. He swerved to avoid it and hit another tree.

"Mr McNeel recovered after staying only five days in hospital. Then he went about his duties, but it was just by sheer will power. He died less than a week after he came home from hospital. There was a very big funeral with over 1000 people in attendance—Hindus, Muslims, and Christians. A public holiday was declared for the funeral and the court closed." Dr Anne Urquhart recorded this fitting tribute in *Near India's Heart*: "John McNeel impressed those who knew him by his obvious devotion to the Lord and by the charm of his personality. His energy and practical abilities were amazing. A memorial booklet published by the Secession Church tells us that he was 'his own architect, his own clerk of works, his own brick-maker, his own contractor, and his own builder. Nothing, in fact, was done except on his advice and under his personal supervision.'"

Both John McNeel and Dr Jeannie Grant enjoyed a considerable interest in Rudyard Kipling who based many of his writings in Central India. 'Council Rock' from Kipling's well-known *Jungle Book* is a good example. In fact, *Mowgli's Song*—"That he sang at the Council Rock when he danced on Shere Khan's hide"— makes reference to the Wainganga River, which flows for part of its course near Chhapara: "Lend me thy coat, Shere Khan. Lend me thy gay striped coat that I may go to the Council Rock... .

Waters of the Wainganga, bear witness that Shere Khan gives me his coat for the love that he bears me." John McNeel wrote to him on one occasion about Council Rock, asking if it was located at Rukhar, between Seoni and Nagpur. Kipling's reply is no longer available, but he is believed to have said that he had never actually located the exact spot himself, but worked from descriptions given to him. We acknowledge with great appreciation the able, willing, and often immediate help which John McNeel gave to Nan and to her colleagues who knew him.

## An Early Furlough

Nan's second term ended in 1955 about nine months prematurely due to the illness of her father. He was still seriously ill when she arrived home in April, but made a reasonable recovery. No doubt, his injuries in the first world war had continued to take their toll. At her Welcome Home the Chairman read a letter from Rev George Sutherland: "This will be a happy occasion for you all, to welcome into your midst one of whom you cannot but feel proud. We cannot, however, but regret that what is your gain is our great loss; you would require to work with Nan in India to realise her worth." George Sutherland was on furlough himself soon after and visited Belfast in September 1955. Nan had been suffering from leg trouble before coming home, and the diagnosis in India was suspected osteomyelitis. However, it turned out to be thrombophlebitis and thankfully it responded to anti-inflammatory treatment and rest while she was at home.

It was in the summer of her 1955 premature furlough that Nan was able to provide the support to her friend Margaret Williamson, now Mrs Leahy, mentioned near the beginning of the story. Mrs

Leahy's mother, Mrs Williamson, had not been well and Mrs Leahy came home from holiday early to be with her, and to allow her sister a few days away. When she learned that the doctor had not been to see her mother recently she sent for him, but he was on holiday and a locum came in his place. The family were not aware of the terminal nature of the diagnosis, and when the locum addressed the matter openly, it was a tremendous shock. That night Nan's sister Lily dreamed that Mrs Williamson was calling for her, and as a result Nan and Lily arrived the next day. Nan found that Mr Williamson was working daily shifts until 2.00 am, and, making up her mind there and then, she stayed with Mrs Leahy until it became clear, within a few days, that Mr Williamson should remain at home. Mrs Williamson died that week. Mrs Leahy still looks back with deep appreciation for what Nan meant to her during those days, not just by her presence in the house, but by the calibre of her spiritual support at a time of personal grief.

We have been conscious that the work of the early 1950's was going on against the background of threat of closure. Major factors pointed to time running out. There was no more appropriate Scripture comment for the impending restriction, it seemed, than the warning of Jesus to His disciples in John 9:4 – "The night cometh when no man can work." But God, in answer to prayer, prolonged the working day. And in the second half of the decade the mood changed. Of course there were trials, setbacks, and disappointments, and the reality of the coming closure remained. But there were renewed opportunities, a new note of encouragement and progress. To this different situation we now turn.

# 8

# Working While it is Day

At her third Valedictory on 23 February 1956, the Foreign Missions Committee of the Free Church of Scotland represented by its Convener, Rev W R Mackay, presented Nan with *The New Bible Commentary* with the wish that she would find it useful in her studies. She set sail for her third term on 2 March 1956 and returned to a warm welcome from "both Christians and non-Christians", bringing her Valedictory offering for much-needed use in the dispensary. She did not take a holiday that year but remained on duty in Chhapara throughout the summer, feeling definitely that this was what the Lord wanted her to do.

## A New Missionary Doctor

Dr Helen Ramsay from the Presbyterian Church of Eastern Australia joined the staff in 1955, increasing the number to six—one minister, two doctors, and three nurses. But more changes were to come within a few years, the first of them in 1957 when Janette Brown returned home. Helen spent her first two years at Lakhnadon, and after language study moved to Chhapara, in anticipation of the expanding medical work there. She pays this tribute to Nan as her mentor during that initial period: "Every new missionary needs a senior to give help and advice in the continuing adjustments to a new culture and a new work.

Nan was my senior and co-worker from 1958, shortly after I finished language study, to 1970. I couldn't have had anyone kinder or easier to live with, nor anyone who was more at home in the Indian way of life. Her Hindi was fluent and idiomatic, and her adaptation to the Indian ways seemed so thorough and effortless that I often wondered if there was an unknown link between the Irish and the Indian."

Coinciding with Dr Helen's arrival in Chhapara, the dispensary building, in use since 1925, was adapted to accommodate four beds for inpatients. Nan did not hide her pleasure at the prospect: "We managed to get some money locally. In fact, the people were very good to us—they want a maternity hospital. From our point of view as well, it is more satisfactory to have patients in hospital for a time. We do not have the same opportunity to speak to outpatients; their minds are usually taken up with the thought of getting home to the children or to the cooking." Sometimes numbers at the dispensary in this period soared to well over 100 a day producing queues, and at times impatience—and even arguments over the smallest of charges.

Helen Ramsay continues her tribute: "Nan had been more than ten years in Chhapara before I came there and was widely known, loved and trusted in the community. She was determined that I too should be accepted but found it difficult. An old lady came to Nan in the hospital after I had examined her. 'Now you look at me,' she said, 'That one didn't even feel my pulse.' So I learnt to feel the pulse even if examining a cut on a foot. When Nan exhorted another patient to take note of what I had said, the answer was: 'An old woman like you knows more than a chit of a girl like her.' For the record Nan is ten

years older than I am and her golden hair was sometimes considered grey! Even a local Government doctor, when Nan advised him to speak to me about a
difficult case, snorted and said: 'What would that
Australian child know?'

"Nan's medical experience impressed me. On a
very early visit to Chhapara I was taken by Nan to a
Brahman house to see a lady who, she thought, had
typhoid. I had never seen a case, so was probably no
help. Nan told them the patient had typhoid. The
other ladies of the house said that she was still sick
because she had not felt well enough to go with
them to visit an idol and do *Puja* to it. So they were
planning to take her in a bullock cart some miles to
this idol. Nan told them that the patient wasn't
strong enough for such a journey and would die if
taken. They took her and she did die."

## Encouragement at the Orphanage

By the mid 1950's the orphanage had seventeen
children of different ages in its care at Chhapara—six
girls and eleven boys. The oldest was Prakash Kumar, now a young man and training as an evangelist
at the Oriental Missionary Society's Bible Seminary
in Allahabad. After completing his first session at the
Bible School, he conducted his first services in
Lakhnadon in the summer of 1955, and continued to
do this whenever he was at home on holiday. Early
in 1957 Nan wrote to the Young People's Bible Class
in her home church, Botanic Avenue: "Prakash, who
is 22, is now taking theological training. He took
most of the services during the two months he was
here. He is a fine lad and taught the little ones Gospel truths in the evenings. I cannot tell you how
much I enjoyed those evenings. I am sure family
prayers lasted well over an hour each evening. The

little ones enjoyed it. We missed Prakash very much after he went back." In 1959 Prakash married Premlata who grew up in the Regions Beyond Missionary Union in North Bihar. She trained as a Bible-woman, also at Allahabad. He was ordained and inducted at Lakhnadon in October 1959 to the ministry of Lakhnadon and Chhapara congregations, and as a measure of the esteem in which he was held in the community, four Hindus attended the service. He was, to use Anne Urquhart's lovely expression, again from *Near India's Heart*, "the first-fruits, so to speak, of the missionaries' efforts to establish a local church."

The summer camp in May 1955 was at Pachmarhi, a hill resort located 3500 feet up in the Satpura mountains, about 150 miles west of Lakhnadon. It was well known for its cool air, streams and pools, and was delightful for walks and relaxation. Nan had several holidays there, as did some of the other missionaries. Taramoni, one of the girls who was deeply influenced at the New Year services in 1948 professed faith at this camp along with another of the orphan girls, Lila. This was during the course of Taramoni's general nursing training at the Bible Churchmen's Missionary Society hospital at Kachhwa, United Provinces—she then went on to do midwifery. Nan remembers on one occasion going back to the hospital with Taramoni by train, in a journey of over 300 miles to the north-west. Nan fell asleep with the result that they missed the station, and had to come back from Benares (now Varanasi). Taramoni was never able to convince Nan that she was asleep too! However, she became a bright Christian and the hospital staff spoke highly of her witness. On her return to Lakhnadon around 1958 she joined the hospital staff and greatly helped the work. Her brother Yunas, often known as 'Innu', became a teacher at the Government Middle School in the mid-1950's. He helped at family worship with the younger children when Prakash returned to the Seminary. Peter and Alexander attended the Vacation Bible School at Pachmarhi in the summer of 1955 and returned with useful notes. They both trained as teachers. Peter and Prembati came to the Lord's Table for the first time in December 1958.

Nan wrote pleasantly in May 1959: "The work among the orphans is encouraging. It was a joy when we asked Peter and Lila to take care of the younger boys in the hot weather, to hear them say, 'Why shouldn't we? We were taken care of when we were small, and it's our family in any case.'" The twins Kamala and Vimala were born at the end of 1958 and joined the orphan family. In June 1960 Nan wrote again about David, the boy who was very attached to her as an infant, but to Nan's lasting regret, she was unable to re-establish the bond with him due to orphanage changes while she was on furlough: "All the children either passed or were promoted in their school examinations, except David. He is a lovely child with a sweet nature, but he does not seem to be able to make the grade at school at all, and I feel so sorry for him." Nan wrote in the spring of 1954 about a boy from Seoni who had taken church services for them recently: "He is very keen and wishes to go out to the villages at night, now that the hot weather is approaching." In her Welcome Home address in May she said that they had been heartened recently by the eagerness of a young Indian evangelist to go out at night and preach in the villages. This was Panna Lal. He married Taramoni and has served the mission as an evangelist and in other roles, continuing beyond the normal retirement age.

Towards the end of Nan's first term, Jharu, after a very promising start, had broken with Christian friends and was resisting all contact. Four years later, in 1953, his wife died after giving birth to another baby, Yunatan. Jharu wanted him brought up a Christian and so he brought him to the mission. Yunatan was ill in May 1957, when he was four, and although he rallied for a time he died. This is how Nan recalls the story: "He was sick and liked to be on your knee. He woke up one night and said, 'Jesus has come, Jesus has come. I'm going to sleep on Jesus' knee'—you could not put that out of his head. He died soon after. The family all came to the funeral. Ashok, another of the orphans, about a year younger than Yunatan, was on my knee. The tears were tripping me. Ashok put his hand into his pocket, took out a small coin, a *paisa,* and pressed it into my hand. Surely that would stop the tears!" Jharu and four other men had come to see Nan a year before this, and they all listened intently as she spoke. He came again two years after Yunatan's death saying that he wanted to come back along with his older boy, but this did not materialise. Jharu never made an open profession again. Nan saw him with his son some years later in Chhapara. She spoke to him about spiritual things and asked him if he had gone back to Hinduism and idol worship. He said that he had not. "Was he a Christian?" Nan was asked later to assess. She replied, "I think he probably was."

**More an Evangelist**
It is impossible to miss the new note of encouragement and potential in Nan's third term correspon-

Working While it is Day

dence on evangelism. One of her first tasks on return in 1956 was to plan with Mary McNeel of Seoni a joint ten-day camp for the older girls to take place in May, fourteen miles beyond Seoni: "There is an old building there without any furniture in it. This we can have without rent. We are taking three of our older orphan girls, and eight of the Seoni orphan girls. The plan is to have Bible Study and do some village work. Do pray for us. Most of the girls are unsaved." The weather was hot for the camp with temperatures as high as 119° (48°), but it was a really good occasion and Nan felt that the girls were genuinely responsive to the morning Bible studies. God blessed the Sunday School work at this time too, and regularly there were over 100 present, including some whose parents had previously forbidden them.

Nan wrote of an exceptionally encouraging day that year. Some of the older boys from a distant village who were in Chhapara to attend the Mission School kept her so engaged with questions about Christ and His cross that she did not manage to start the prescribed lesson. It would have been a rare privilege to listen in on that discussion on "Christ and him crucified." To many of those lads the cross was, and has remained, foolishness; perhaps to some of them Christ has or will even yet become the power and the wisdom of God.

A journey Nan made to an outlying village in the monsoons of that year gives a little insight into the dangers and discomfort the missionaries willingly accepted: "I had to go to one village five miles away on horseback, then across the swollen river in a canoe—a small one cut out of the trunk of a tree. There was a lot of water in the bottom of the boat, so I sat on a walking-stick just put across the top. There were two women and the boatman with me, and when we sat down the water was less than an inch off the top—a little more and we would have been at the bottom of the river. The horse after some persuasion—and not gentle persuasion!—swam across."

Sometimes the stories are particularly sad: "The people listen quite well to the Gospel, but the tragedy is that it seems to go 'in one ear and out the other.' One poor woman, when her baby got a little better (he had been very ill), went off to a shrine to worship, taking the baby with her. She said the goddess had asked for the baby's new shirt and his jersey as a thank-offering. I'm sure buying the jersey at the first meant a struggle to her."

In January 1957 Nan attended a conference in Calcutta with George Sutherland and her friend Mary McNeel from Seoni. Dr Akbar Abdul Haqq, a convert from Islam, was the speaker and gave a series of messages which Nan found very inspiring. Soon after she expressed regret that there were not more resources to work "while it is yet day": "The Sutherland family, Dr Ramsay and I were at camp for two and a half months this winter and had a good time. The people in most of the villages listened well to the messages, and wanted us to stay and open a dispensary among them. I was very sorry that was not possible, for the Roman Catholics seem to be busy in that direction." In June of the same year Nan was able to continue the spiritual nourishment and fellowship at a ten-day break at Mussoorie in the hills for a nurses' camp. Poor bookings were the only disappointment.

During a winter camp of this period in the Narsinghpur direction, George Sutherland, Dr Annie Mackay, Mary MacDonald and Nan were out doing village evangelism. George and Dr Annie crossed a stream with bicycles to visit a village and Mary and Nan stayed with the *chakra* (bullock cart). Then the rain came on and Nan remembers it as heavy even by Indian standards. In a short time the river was in flood, but George and Dr Annie were able to wade back over to where the others were waiting with the *chakra*. The chakra normally seats its passengers one behind the other, but this one had been specially constructed for the mission, with a double cushioned seat in front and a raised wooden bench behind. Dr Annie was drenched and Nan said to her: "You get in here beside Mary." When Nan got up on to the bench at the back the two bullocks were unable to move the cart through the soft ground. So she got down, and describing herself as a 'drowned rat' walked to a bus route. The driver stopped for her— and then another problem—she had no money! However, her destination was not far, and the conductor gave her a free trip. When she got back to the camp site Godwin and Charan, the cook, were hammering the pegs of the Sutherlands' tent into the ground to keep it standing. While they were doing that, the tent where the dinner, normally cooked outside, was being made, collapsed on top of it all. George meanwhile was wheeling the bicycles back!

On another occasion they were camping near Kahani, and George Sutherland was out in the jeep with Nan, Helen and his children on village visits. Someone came asking for a doctor and Helen said she would go. George decided to accompany them and asked Nan to drive the children home. He put the jeep into 2nd gear for Nan and told her not to change gear all the way home as the ground was rough and wet. When they got back, one of the little girls said: "If anyone didn't know you were just learning, they would give you a B+!" At another camp at this time near Kahani Mary MacDonald was alone in her tent writing letters. Prakash and his wife had a tent close by. Mary heard noises around her tent and thought she should investigate, but then decided just to leave it. The next day the people said: "Did you not see the tiger at your tent last night?" The pug marks were there to prove it.

Nan's desire for the personal evangelistic role became more and more apparent during these years, as we see in a letter towards the end of 1958: "The hospital at Chhapara is still busy—usually there are over 100 out-patients each morning apart from in-patients. I find the people more willing than ever before to take literature. I have more time to talk to them these days, for I seem to be more an evangelist than anything else, now that we have Dr Ramsay and Taramoni, one of our orphans who is a trained nurse." And again in the same year as they planned for another camp: "There are school holidays from today for 24 days; so Panna will be free and we can have Panna and Prakash. Both lads are keen to win souls. Last Friday we went in search of a camping site and found one twelve-fourteen miles from here, in a village where there is a school and a lot of children. The children were very keen to listen to us on Friday, and I believe a grand work could be done among them. The village seemed a fairly prosperous one and the children intelligent. We would very much like a lot of prayer support. It will be the first time for Panna and Prakash to camp. We have made very little impression on this particular area yet. Why should the devil keep his goods in peace? I believe he won't if we all pray and God blesses our witness."

**Sickness and Bereavement**

One of the greatest sacrifices the missionary calling requires is prolonged absence from home and family. News of bereavement while absent from the family circle is particularly hard to bear. Nan's father, Hugh Dunlop, died on 17 March 1959, three years after she last saw him. As we know, his health had been poor for a number of years and he had realised for some time that his earthly life was drawing to a close. He often looked forward to his eternal rest, speaking with delight of the things of God. A few weeks before his death he asked Rev W J Grier to pass on the message to Nan in India that he died happy, trusting in the Lord, and looking for the glad reunion.

Nan also continued to have her share of sickness. Early in 1958 she had kidney trouble and was confined to bed for some weeks. She went to Nagpur for blood tests and X-rays. In May of the following year it was an attack of jaundice, but its timing fitted in well with her annual holiday in the hills where she was able to recuperate. It is strange how some severe sickness, all of it affecting her feet and legs, afflicted Nan just before each of her first three furloughs. At the end of her first term it was poison in her leg caused when a graze in her heel became infected as she walked through the mud. Just before she came home for her second furlough, she was suffering from leg trouble again—this time, thrombophlebitis.

After her summer holidays in May 1959, Nan moved to Lakhnadon, again to provide cover at the hospital when Dr Annie was on furlough. Less than three months later she wrote the letter which appears as chapter 1 of this book. How much in demand she was at the time, and how greatly she looked forward to her furough, still more than eighteen months away! Her move to Lakhnadon left Helen alone at Chhapara and Nan wrote of her feeling about it: "I have been alone before and she has not. It is not easy—so please remember us specially." George Sutherland resigned and returned to Scotland in October 1959, which re-opened the quest for a minister to superintend the mission. With Dr Annie on furlough and Mary MacDonald on sick leave this left only Nan and Helen on the field, but in Prakash they now had an ordained minister.

In July 1960, as she entered the last six months of her third term she became critically ill with the effects of snake-bite to her foot. She wrote: "Last Sunday morning as I sat reading in the garden, something bit me. I did not see what it was. I only saw the spot of blood after it was gone and I thought nothing of it. About two hours later I had such a rigor and then a temperature of over 103°. I never thought to mention the bite and so was treated for malaria. At 4.00 pm I remembered the bite and sent to Lakhnadon for Dr Annie Mackay and Nurse MacDonald. By the time they came the foot was swelling and discoloured and I was very ill. All the Indian folk say it was snake-bite or I would not have turned blue." The *Irish Evangelical* of September 1960 goes on: "When her illness was at its height the words of the 23rd Psalm were of great comfort to her. Also, the words of the Psalmist in the 118th Psalm came to her heart with power: 'I shall not die, but live, and declare the works of the Lord.' She was still very ill on the following Monday and Tuesday, but by Thursday she was considerably better, but even on the Friday her foot was still swollen, and she was being treated with penicillin and achromycin. She has been brought to the gates of death but the Lord has helped her and in a measure restored her. May she be strengthened in body and profit in spirit from this experience of God's presence and His goodness."

Each of the missionaries suffered in some way from illness as we see from a brief scan of the later 1950's alone. Mary MacDonald had to go home, seriously ill with hepatitis, in November 1958, accompanied by Dr Annie. Dr Annie was unwell herself in 1955 after her return from furlough and was advised by her Nagpur specialist to rest. George Sutherland had a breakdown in health in 1957. Helen Ramsay developed jaundice in 1959 about the same time as Nan did. It happened just after a village camp, from which Helen made the journey back to Chhapara every day to do the morning dispensary. The camp site was three miles off the road and the track was so bad that she had to walk. Perhaps the strenuous physical exertion every day predisposed her to the attack—Nan felt it did. Dr Annie had an accident in the jeep late in 1960 when travelling back from Seoni with Tarabai. They both sustained injuries, Dr Annie's being the more serious. Each decade of missionary service was marked by similar trial.

Tiwari had his own grief to bear too. We last met Daya, his youngest son, in 1949, when he was sixteen. He was a rather wild lad and by then had already run away from home on several occasions. Daya died in December 1958. Tiwari told Nan that he had been reading the Bible for three months before he died and that he had come to personal faith in Christ. He was to have requested baptism at Christmas. Nan felt that in the light of his way of life until then, his reading of the Bible was certainly evidence of change. After his service in Kahani Tiwari moved to the *Toriya* in Lakhnadon until he retired in

1966, over 70 years of age. He spent his last few years with his eldest son Jyotish in Maharashtra. Daya had two sons, Sant Pal and Jai Pal, who lived and moved with Tiwari during these years. They were well known at the mission during their time at Lakhnadon. Tiwari also had a daughter, Sarajoni, who trained as a nurse and moved to another area. And here we conclude the Tiwari story. He kept his vow and never crossed the river between the *Toriya* and Lakhnadon again. We thank God for saving him, for the bond which existed between him and Nan, and for everything he did and bore for the cause of Christ in Chhapara and in the villages of the mission territory.

## Reading Rooms and School

Social changes brought more opportunities too. A Reading Room was opened in Chhapara to try to reach the teachers at the new government Teachers' Training College near the mission buildings: "We hope that many of them will come in the evenings, and so we are trying to stock the room with suitable books in Hindi. Pray also for this new venture, and for Peter, one of our Christian boys, who will be more or less in charge of the work. He will need a great deal of wisdom in speaking to any who come along. It is a wonderful opportunity to reach these young people, who are preparing to go out and teach in the government schools." Speaking of those teachers over 40 years later, Nan recalled: "A lot of those men would come in to me and I would give them tea. On quite a few occasions they would be sitting round the wall and maybe take the Gospel for an hour. And they all went away with New Testaments and other pieces of literature back to their own villages." This Reading Room was the forerunner of the 'Elizabeth Macleod Memorial Reading Room' which was opened in a new building beside the school in 1964.

In Lakhnadon, by the end of the 1950's there were increased numbers of government officials who could speak English to add to a growing number of the new generation who were educated and wanted to read. Prompted by this potential, Nan and Dr Helen wrote to Dr Annie at home on furlough, proposing a Reading Room in the vestry of Lakhnadon church, ideally placed beside the bus depot in the heart of the village. It was all agreed and the facility was made available throughout the 1960's. The mission also started a Sunday service at Ghansore, 21 miles east of Lakhnadon, for the families of a few government employees there who were Christians.

Yet another responsibility of Nan's during these years was the Mission School: "I have charge of the school now too—about 235 children. We have Panna, our evangelist, teaching in the school and taking the Bible lessons. It is wonderful to have the opportunity of working with so many young lives. Do pray for the work done in the school. Panna is very good with the children and is a real evangelist." The government Training College used the Mission School for their students' practicals.

**Another Missionary Arrives**

In 1960 Mervyn Oliver, a deacon from Nan's home congregation, applied to the Foreign Missions Committee as an unordained missionary and was accepted. He sailed on 2 April 1960. Nan sent an assertive, confident letter which was read at his valedictory service. She was clearly in good heart: "Good for the Irish Evangelical Church. It's doing well." She went on to warn of the renowned difficulty of Christian witness in Madyha Pradesh, but countered boldly with the promise: "There is nothing too hard for the Lord." She then asked for prayer for the first Daily Vacation Bible School, planned for October, for the children of the mission school: "The children do have religious instruction every day but we feel the need of something more—perhaps the need for decision must be brought more forcibly to them." In closing she recalled the story of a policeman, a former pupil of the school, whom they had met quite recently in Jabalpur. He told them of his conviction of sin and conversion, ten years before, and many years after he had left school. His family had disowned him and he had to leave, but he said that he could do no other. Nan said this: "The Lord's promise holds true—'your labour is not in vain in the Lord.' There are the drops, but we long to see showers. It is possible through your prayers."

Mervyn went to Language School at Landour in 1960 and to Allahabad in 1961. Nan was able to visit him in the summer of 1960 at Landour on her way back from holiday in Kashmir. Mervyn's letters could be quite descriptive, and at Landour he observed: "It is such a change from the hot, thirsty plains. Even at 7000 feet the sun is very much in evidence, and we are glad when a cool breeze blows to temper the heat. Away to the north, standing guard over India, we can see the snow-covered Himalayan peaks. Down in the south the plains are usually shrouded in a haze of heat. In between, we are perched on the tree-covered hillside."

**Concluding the Third Term**

Nan and Mary McNeel left Bombay on furlough together on 10th March 1961. They had decided to go by sea as far as Naples, and then to travel home through Europe by train. Among the passengers on the ship to Naples was a party of Jesuit priests who provided a question-box for passengers to submit topics for discussion in open forum at appointed times. One of them invited Nan to visit Clonard monastery in Belfast! Nan and Mary had bought some Travellers Cheques at Bombay, but it was only on arrival in Italy that they discovered the stamp on the back of each of them, 'Only negotiable in the United Kingdom.' During their short say at Naples they saw Vesuvius and went on a day-trip to Sorrento.

They arrived at Rome nearly penniless and were perplexed about what to do. After some discussion they presented themselves at the Church of Scotland manse and found that the minister was also a representative of the British Embassy. Expectantly they asked if they could cash their cheques through the Embassy, but the answer was that the Embassy could only treat them as 'Distressed British Subjects' and arrange to get them home in the cheapest possible way! However the minister gave them a warm reception and provided them with two nights accommodation in his beautiful manse. He was able to lend them £10.00 which they later returned to his bank account in the UK. He was extremely helpful, advising them where to shop, and how to get around by bus. One of his useful tips was that they should not to sit down at a table in a restaurant, but stand at the counter where it would cost much less. Nan and Mary climbed the steps of St Peter's. They visited the Colosseum where the Roman gladiators fought, and where some of the early Christians were killed by lions; and the Catacombs, the underground chambers and passages dug as hiding places by the Christians at Rome during times of persecution.

Crossing the Alps into Switzerland they were awake to see a spectacular dawn, and it has remained with Nan as a vivid memory. They stayed for a night at the Geneva Salvation Army Hostel, having got there at the second attempt. Their taxi driver had taken first to a home for down and outs! Their last stop was Paris before they boarded the ferry at Calais, for Dover and home.

Nan's Welcome Home after her 3rd term of service was held on 13 April 1961. She spoke particularly about the orphans and thanked the church for their continual intercession which had enabled her to overcome the dangers and difficulties she had faced. Letters were read from two of her colleagues in India, Dr Annie and Mervyn Oliver, in which they stressed the need for her to rest, hoping that the church would not impose too great a deputation burden upon her.

During her furlough Nan spoke at the Clintyfallow church conference in Tyrone in May where she took the opportunity of presenting India's still-open door and the consequent pressing need for more missionaries now. She encouraged her hearers with evidence that God had already honoured the preaching and teaching of His word. A few weeks later she addressed the General Assembly in Edinburgh and again she made the case for India's urgent missionary need. Miss Flora Macleod was present at that Assembly and remembers Nan's visit well: "I had heard about Nan Dunlop since I was a little girl, from my mother. Once I was accepted by the Foreign Missions Committee for India in 1962, I then met Nan face to face, as she spoke at the General Assembly and I thought to myself, 'Well she seems a lot of fun and what a tremendous speaker she is, but I hope I never have to speak at the General Assembly!'" Nan always did deputation work in Scotland during her furloughs and on this occasion she was there twice—in November 1961 and February 1962. The congregation of Dingwall Free Church kindly held her 'Scottish' valedictory.

It is a strange phenomenon that missionaries from the same church who work in different mission fields and who might profit from meeting to share the experiences of their common calling may be deprived of seeing one another for extended periods, if their furloughs do not overlap. Nan experienced this loss with regard to Joseph and Helen McCracken, the missionaries who left for South Africa in the same convoy as she had done at the end of 1944, and also with Florrie Donaldson, from her own congregation, who went to Peru in 1951. The McCrackens and Florrie Donaldson were both due home in March 1962, and with Nan not scheduled to leave until the end of March it looked as if they would see one another for a short time. Florrie Donaldson arrived as planned at the beginning of March, but in a letter received in February Mr McCracken, explaining that they had just opened two new churches, announced: "We feel we cannot leave the work at this stage." Their furlough was delayed until 1963.

It is a matter for continuing and particular thankfulness that the attitudes at the beginning of the 1950's which threatened the future of mission work in India were not put into early effect as they might have been. More time was needed and God gave it. Missionary opportunity continued until 1988. By then, the youngest orphan was nineteen, the Free Church of Central India was established, and the medical work incorporated into the Emmanuel Hospital Association, perhaps the largest indigenous medical mission in the world. Chhapara Mission School had also grown to nearly 600 pupils divided into Kindergarten, Primary, and Middle sections. We have seen that Nan's own mood changed quite markedly during the period. Near the beginning there was the note of strong discouragement in the face of active opposition and rebuff. But from the middle of the 50's there was a change. Gloom gave place to buoyancy as fresh opportunities arose in every part of the work. Throughout the period the boldness and effectiveness of the missionaries in communicating the Gospel were striking. It is still remarkable that the increase was so small, but so God ordered it as He has on many occasions in the history of His church. He does not work in the same way among all people at all times. Nan herself adopted a greater evangelistic role during her third term. As we turn now to the fourth we will see a further and very significant adjustment to her range of responsibilities.

## 9

## "Mother to our Orphan Children"

When Nan arrived in India in April 1962 to commence her 4th term she had come to the half-way point of her missionary career. Very often the second half seems to pass more quickly and this case was not an exception. In many ways the work and the methods continued to the end as they were when she went in 1944, but while change was slow, it was far more significant in the second fifteen years than it was in the first. During her 30 years Nan had fifteen missionary colleagues in all. Of these, six began their careers during her first three terms and six during the second three; the others were on the field before her. Her longest partnership by far—22 years—was with Dr Annie Mackay. It is in the second half too, that we see more of Nan in the work with which she is most associated. Anne Urquhart identifies it in *Near India's Heart*: "Capable nurse and midwife though she is, it is as a teller of 'the old, old story' and as mother to our orphan children that she is best remembered."

Nan's Belfast valedictory was held on 22 March 1962. Rev A MacDougall and Rev George Sutherland represented the Free Church. Rev MacDougall laid before the congregation for prayer and consideration one of the pressing needs of the mission at the time and one which was to remain on the agenda for almost another three years—a minister to take the place of Rev George Sutherland, now ministering at home. Mr Sutherland, drawing on his own first hand experience, told of the influence Nan exercised on the field. He described her as a versatile missionary who never lost sight of the fact that she had a Gospel to proclaim. Rev A A Campbell, current chairman of Council (soon to be Presbytery) of the Irish Evangelical Church, addressed Nan from Judges 6:14: "Go in this thy might... have not I sent thee," and from Joshua 1:9: "Have not I commanded thee? Be strong and of a good courage; be not afraid, neither be thou dismayed: for the Lord thy God is with thee whithersoever thou goest."

She took back boxes of supplies for the hospital. Very often customs regulations and procedures can be frustrating and subject to delay, as Nan was to find in another context three years later, but the authorities at Bombay treated her with great consideration in her task of securing the transfer of the boxes to Lakhnadon. En route from Bombay, thirteen of the precious boxes disappeared for a time and the signs did not look good, but eventually they all turned up intact. Missionary travellers had a lot to contend with in those days.

**The New Chhapara Reading Room**

Nan resumed work in Chhapara and her first subject of correspondence in the new term was the Reading Room: "Some of the lads who come to the reading-room asked if we had a Bible Class on Sundays. They are non-Christians and desire help for they don't understand what they read. One asked for an English Bible; another wanted to buy a Hindi Bible." By this time plans for the new reading room—The Elizabeth Macleod Memorial Reading Room—were well advanced, but implementation was another matter. Nan wrote in July 1962 of the problems: "Pray for the preparation of the new reading-room. There are difficulties in plenty. Cement is only obtainable by permit from the district commissioner. There is so much building going on at the moment that wood, bricks, tiles, labour, etc, are at peak prices." Anne Urquhart described the effective interest Nan had taken in the new Reading Room during her deputation visits to Scotland during her last furlough: "Nan Dunlop, on home leave in 1962, was so persuasive in encouraging people to give money for the Reading Room that it was whispered she should be detained in Scotland to work on behalf of the Sustentation Fund!" This was the fund for paying ministers' stipends. Correspondence during 1965 recorded that the average daily attendance at the new reading room was around 100. Prakash was staffing the facility during opening hours, working with Nan who was providing a guiding hand. Between February, when the new reading room was opened, and the end of the year, over 5,000 signed the visitors' book. About 100 of the users were doing Bible Correspondence Courses, some of them assisted by Prakash. Good books were urgently needed to develop the potential of the work, and Nan noted receipt of 100 new ones in February of the following year.

## The 4th Term Staff Changes

As we keep abreast of Nan's colleagues we first return to Mervyn Oliver. At the end of 1961 he became engaged to Miss Pat Hearn whom he met at Landour when he was studying language there earlier in the year. They were married in 1963, and at the end of that year Mervyn left the mission, after giving six months' notice, to join the Swedish Lu-

*Service in a Sari*

theran Mission who also worked in Madhya Pradesh. There were four new missionaries in Nan's 4th term. Dr Anne Urquhart, a niece of Dr Annie Mackay, and Flora Macleod, a nurse, arrived together in August 1962, just four months after Nan returned from furlough. Anne Urquhart was from Killearnan in the Black Isle in Ross-shire, and Flora Macleod from Edinburgh. They served until 1984 and 1975 respectively. During the time that Nan and Dr Anne were on the field together Anne worked at the hospital in Lakhnadon. Flora Macleod was with Nan at Chhapara until 1968, the first year of Nan's 5th term, when she moved to Lakhnadon. Miss Heather Beaton, sent by the Presbyterian Church of Eastern Australia, Newcastle, New South Wales, and also a nurse, came the following year, and like Anne Urquhart she worked at Lakhnadon during the remaining years of Nan's service.

Anne Urquhart recalls a couple of early experiences where Nan held centre stage: "Returning from Language School, a group of us had enjoyed seeing Delhi and the Taj Mahal. But our rupees were running out as we travelled (I had foolishly bought a cool cotton *sari*—pale pinks, blues and whites—on the way). The coolies at Nagpur Railway Station mobbed us but soon turned very angry when we protested that we were almost broke. Nan, meeting us, brought down their demands, paid them, then took us, ravenous as we were, for a good meal. Talk about coming to the rescue!" Anne tells also how Nan soon came to the rescue again, but this time in other circumstances: "Doctors are notoriously bad patients. I was *not* ready to admit that I had acute appendicitis... ." Nan interrupts at this point to tell more of the story: "I wanted to send to Lakhnadon for Dr Annie, but Anne wouldn't hear of it. I took her pulse and asked, 'What would you say to anyone who had a pulse of 130?' She said, 'I would say they had a foetal heart!' But I sent for Dr Annie anyway." Anne goes on: "Nan it was who bundled me into the car for the Mure Memorial Hospital in Nagpur. The first I knew on regaining consciousness was her soothing but firm tones, telling me not to disturb the intravenous drip... ." Flora MacLeod (now Mrs Neil, and living in Australia) recalls from the same time: "Nan and I were in Chhapara for my first six weeks before Anne Urquhart and I went to Language School in Allahabad. It was wonderful being with Nan then and she really gave me a great welcome along with the Indians, and helped me through those early days, telling me what one does or doesn't do, eg, going into an Indian house without taking off one's shoes. When you arrive in a foreign country you do become homesick and wait eagerly for letters from home (Scotland), and Nan would have lots of tales to keep us amused—both Irish and Indian."

Rev Ian McKenzie, another Australian, was ordained in 1964 in Edinburgh after study at the Free Church College, and appointed Mission Superintendent in India, five years after George Sutherland had resigned. He served for twenty years until 1984. Nan described the part she played in his arrival, which involved an experience with the Customs that was less happy than in 1962 when she herself was disembarking with the boxes of hospital supplies: "At Christmas Rev Ian McKenzie arrived and, as the Customs detained some of his baggage, I had to go to Bombay in January. It took me nearly three weeks to clear the detained packages, most of which contained clothes for free distribution. It was amazing the number of obstructions the Customs put in the way of clearing the goods. But the sustaining promises of the Lord during those days were, 'The Lord thy God, he it is that doth go before thee' and 'He will silently plan for thee'—and He did in a wonderful way. Praise His name!" In 1966 Rev McKenzie married Alina Murchinson from Alness in Ross-shire. The wedding was at Lakhnadon and they lived there until 1968 when they moved to Chhapara, and to closer contact with Nan. Alina remembers their first wedding anniversary when Nan was with them and they had a moonlit picnic on the banks of the Wainganga river: "We sat and ate Heather Beaton's wonderful Lamingtons!" These are squares of sponge cake coated with chocolate and coconut—a delicacy of Australia.

A landmark in the history of the Indian mission was reached early in 1966 with the retirement of Dr Annie Mackay after 45 years' service. Nan was leaving on furlough at the same time and accompanied her on the journey home. For a retirement present she had decided on one of the pictures which local artists paint on the metal griddles used for baking *chapattis*, and some of the other missionaries went with them as far as Jabalpur to help her to choose it. Nan saw a picture which she thought Dr Annie might like, and as she began to carry it into the other room of the shop where Dr Annie was having a look, a dog, believing he was dealing with a thief, caught her by the leg and bit her. Nan needed antirabies injections which continued during the train journey to Bombay.

It would be remiss to conclude our references to the missionary life of Dr Annie Mackay without some comment on her remarkable commitment to village visitation. She maintained meticulous, hand-written, daily records of her programme, with dates, village names and various running totals. It was very moving to find among the pages of her 1941-1966 register, a little note referring to the village of Katkuhi, in the Nursinghpur district, north-west of Lakhnadon. She had written: "Last new village visited." And she had numbered it 389, the highest new village number in her records. It was dated 25.10.65 — just a few months before she retired.

Dr Annie was blessed with a long and fruitful retirement. She celebrated her 100th birthday on 16 January 1993 and went to be with the Lord less than one year later on 9 December. Various tributes to her wonderful life's work, which we have only touched on in these pages, have appeared in her church's magazine, *The Monthly Record of the Free Church of Scotland*.

## Unexpected Breaks

Nan's 4th term had two significant breaks. The first of these came in March 1963 when Flora Macleod, after less than eight months on the field, became ill, and had to return to Scotland urgently for treatment and rest. Nan flew home with her, her first journey home by air, and was able to stay for a month in Belfast doing deputation work around the churches and spending time with her family. Her account of the arrangements for bringing Flora home and the events leading up to it are full of interest. Dr Misra, a specialist from the Medical College at Jabalpur, arrived at Chhapara to see Flora on the day of the annual *Holi* spring festival, the most flamboyant and exuberant of all the Hindu festivals. In the morning, to set the day's activities in motion, the people throw coloured water and brightly coloured powder at each other. There is quite a bit of running and chasing. Children target teachers and workers go for managers. As Dr Misra walked along the street with Dr

Helen Ramsay, the men of the village moved to drench him with colour, but Helen stopped them with a word. Dr Misra acknowledged with surprise and admiration that it was the first time he had been protected by a woman—and with such authority!

Nan and Dr Helen set off for Chhindwara to get clearance for Flora to go home. Income Tax and some other formalities had to be confirmed up to date before anyone could leave. While there, they decided to visit Shaw Wallace, a company with mining and other business interests, who were located at Parasia, a further 25 miles north-west of Chhindwara. The missionaries knew of Shaw Wallace through a visit its representatives had made to the mission on behalf of the British Embassy, to check that all was well at a time of tension in the area. The chief mining engineer was Mr McNeill, a Scotsman, and the chief surveyor, an Englishman Mr Slater. They provided greatly needed help and relief that day when the two burdened lady missionaries called with them to seek advice, and Nan and Helen saw it as the Lord's own providential provision. Mr McNeill managed to get through to Bombay by telephone, often a formidable and frustrating task. He made the travel bookings and arranged for Flora to stay in a private hospital until her flight was leaving. He then sent an ambulance from Parasia to Chhapara to take her, with Helen and Nan, to Nagpur, for the train journey to Bombay. The Company even assisted with Helen's return journey, organising her transfer to the railway station at Bombay where she found a packed lunch and a basket of fruit awaiting her. The occasion brought the mission into closer relationship with Shaw Wallace who later helped with advice and supervision of building projects.

But we allow Flora to resume the story: "I did become ill at the beginning of 1963 and eventually had to be flown home. However before that I think I gave all the missionaries who were looking after me in Chhapara a few extra grey hairs—Dr Annie Mackay, Dr Helen Ramsay and Nan. When after some weeks it was decided to fly me home, it was Nan who went with me. One thing that sticks out in my mind is that when we were caught in a sandstorm in Arabia, and the hostess told Nan that everyone was to leave the plane, except Nan and myself, I remember it going through my mind 'I wonder what will happen to us!' But I was given peace in my heart, and knew God our heavenly father was watching over us." These storms could last several hours or several days, but graciously this one was just hours. However, the travellers were delayed enough to miss their train connection to Edinburgh from London, and Flora was admitted to a London hospital overnight. Thankfully her recovery was speedy and she returned to India within six months. She concluded her short account: "It was wonderful to rejoin Nan in India in September 1963."

The second journey home for Nan was two years later in April 1965 when her mother became ill. On hearing the news she hurried the 600 miles to Bombay and again came home by air. As with the previous break, Nan was at home for about a month, and took the opportunity to go round the churches. Her mother improved considerably before she left.

## The Medical Work Expands

The medical work continued, gradually expanding its services through additional staff and equipment, and in 1964, for the first time in her correspondence, Nan began to write about eye operations, which

Helen Ramsay carried out, often in exhausting temperatures. She wrote in March: "Dr Helen Ramsay is doing quite a number of eye operations these days, and it's lovely to go and speak to the patients. They seem so responsive." She had more to say in April: "One of our eye patients said tonight, when Dr Ramsay was urging them not to forget what she had been telling them: 'No, indeed, haven't I been praying night and morning in Jesus' name since my first operation.' The eye-patients are wonderful listeners. One young woman was totally blind—she had never seen her small son who is four years old. It was very touching to witness the scene the first day she was able to see the child."

We have already noted the upgrading of the Chhapara dispensary in 1957 to accommodate a small number of in-patients. At Lakhnadon, the arrival of the new doctor and the two new nurses in 1962-63 provided the basis to develop the medical services there. So in 1966 the hospital Inpatient facility was increased to 24 by the addition of two new wards and the incorporation of the out-patient department. This was a big step forward from the situation in 1944, when Nan arrived, when there were just five beds. In February 1966 she commented typically on some of the practical difficulties: "The work on the hospital at Lakhnadon has not been started yet. We are waiting for Mr Slater. Cement has been de-controlled and the price is going up." Mr Slater was of course the chief surveyor from the mining company, Shaw Wallace, who were of such memorable help during Flora MacLeod's journey home on sick leave in 1963. His company's advice and assistance were again on offer.

A new ambulance and trailer arrived from Scotland in March 1966. Nan wrote in anticipation of it, with a note that inspires our retrospective confidence: "Heather and I go to Bombay next Thursday to bring back the new ambulance (and trailer). It will take ages to bring it back. It's a long, long way and it will be 'running in.' We don't know the way back, but we shall find it by the map." We are glad of Heather Beaton's confirmation that they did: "On one memorable occasion I accompanied Nan to Bombay to collect a Land Rover Ambulance which had arrived from UK. Before leaving Nagpur we had been given some good advice by an English businessman, who also said we could use his name in the event of major difficulties. We stayed at a Salvation Army guest house quite close to the Port area and met folk who told gloomy stories of how long it would take to clear a vehicle. Some had to remain in Bombay six to eight weeks. We also met a friendly young man from Somerset, who was returning home after spending almost a year studying the ways of Australian farming in Queensland.

"Bombay wharves seem to extend for miles, and along these miles Nan and I were sent hither and thither daily. The wharves were distinguished by colour codes. After examining our documents we would be referred to the Blue wharf, only to be told by an official that for a certain signature we must return to the Red wharf. Perhaps the officer we needed to see would be off duty that day etc, etc. More than once in sheer frustration, even Nan's patience wore thin, and with a stamp of her dainty foot, and the mention of our Nagpur friend's name, we would be in possession of the signature and the magic mauve stamp of approval, and off to conquer the next hurdle. Finally after only eleven days the vehicle was pushed off the wharf into the street, and we helped push it a little further along the street for fuel.

"But... that was not all. The 'last rite' before leaving Bombay had to be performed when the vehicle was checked out mechanically, by the 'right' people. We prayed that the new Land Rover would not be the worse for these ministrations. Our friend from Somerset, who proved to be a competent driver, went with us on this occasion, and spent an interesting day observing. We had noticed a lovely car on the wharves, which was destined to be owned by the King of Nepal. This car was given a thorough going over by staff who spent a great deal of time applying grease and oil to its door hinges. The object of this exercise was to eliminate a certain 'click' in the doors. The 'click' of course was built in to prevent the car doors swinging wide open in one movement. Hopefully the King's car also received the stamp of approval. Our Somerset friend said he couldn't believe his eyes most of the time, and spent a very interesting day. Nan explained to him how important it had been for us to have a male standing by apparently supervising check-out procedures. The Land Rover and trailer were eventually cleared of *all* red tape at 4.30 pm, and we set off. Our young friend readily accepted Nan's invitation to accompany us as far as Nagpur and share the driving.

"Not far out on the road in a nearby town we lost the main highway turning, and passed through some hilly and very scenic countryside. We stopped at dusk to offer a couple of men a lift, only to find that one was a prisoner and handcuffed to a policeman. We dropped them at the police station, accepted a cup of tea, and received good instructions for our outward journey, and where we could obtain accommodation in a nearby village.

"The next day we travelled on. The weather was very hot, and I remember visiting railway refreshment rooms, drinking 'gallons' of tea, filling all available flasks and bottles with boiled water, and even managing to take a shower. On arrival in Nagpur, late afternoon, we dined in Kwality restaurant and saw our friend on to the train to return to Bombay. The next day after the last hundred miles of the journey we were given a great welcome in Lakhnadon/Chhapara. When one official at Bombay showed surprise at what we had achieved in eleven days, Nan informed him that we had the Lord on our side. His answer was 'I wish I had him on my side.'"

## Babies at the Orphanage

Dr Anne Urquhart in a circular letter from Chhapara in September 1965 wrote very significantly of Nan: "Although her main concern is with the children—and that has included recently supervision of repairs to their house—she has a guiding hand on the school and Reading Room too." We have already drawn attention more than once to a change in Nan's role towards the end of the 1950's giving her more time for direct evangelism. Here we come to another change—a concentration on orphan care. Neither of these adjustments meant the cessation of medical work, for Nan continued her nursing and midwifery duties around the villages and in the dispensary throughout her career, but they did mean that her main responsibilities had shifted to the orphans by the middle of her 4th term. Here, her nursing skills had special application.

Several new orphans joined the family in 1962-63 making 1963 a suitable year to take stock: First there was Ashok who was nine, then the twin girls Kamala and Vimala now five, and the baby boys, whose photographs, taken about 1970, appear on the front cover—Arun and Santosh, born in 1962, and Vinai, Vijai, and Sharan in 1963. Kiran, a girl, not in the cover photograph, was also born in 1963. This was a family of ten of whom five were babies, all under Nan's care. During this time Nan had all five small babies in her own bedroom. In July of that year, speaking of the four babies who had arrived at the time of writing, she said: "the care of them is a full-time job." Helen Ramsay agrees: "When we had the five orphan babies in the house Nan devoted herself to them and to the many humble tasks that accompanied this care. At the hottest time of the year she stayed with them while the rest of us were on holiday."

Sometimes the care of an orphan gave witnessing contact with the child's father as Nan described in March 1964: "The father of one of the babies under our care almost always asks for new literature when he visits us. He says his son reads all he gets to the people in the village." Then there was an interesting night in December 1964 when the babies made one of their annual visits to evangelistic camp: "Dr Urquhart, Miss Macleod, Rev Prakash and I were at camp. Dr Urquhart and Miss Macleod did medical work—Dr Urquhart using her Hindi very nicely to speak to the people before giving them treatment. Prakash went off in the mornings to villages. I did not get out during the day—we had five babies with us and there was washing, bathing, feeding, etc—but we all went to the village in which we camped every night after dinner... ." It may have been from an evening at this camp that Anne Urquhart remembers this very special story: "The raw recruit didn't understand the local dialect, but from Nan's vigorous gestures I knew she was explaining clearly the wonder of Jesus' death and resurrection, as we sat round the camp fire at Sahajpuri. She rescued me from a sticky situation the next day. Unwittingly, looking round the camp-fire group, my eye must have caught that of someone sitting opposite. (I learned later that good women do not let their eyes wander like that). Nan had to assure the young man that... no, I was not on the marriage market!" But Nan resumes: "We had one exciting night out there when the rain flooded us almost out, and the tent fell down on all the babies' clothes, beds, bedding, etc. When Dr Urquhart tried to bring the jeep out to take the babies to safety, it stuck in the mud—so we waited until morning, and carrying a baby each we walked the two miles through the mud to the main road. I had to keep the babies at home for a week as they all developed bad colds." The next February the children received some generous and unexpected gifts: "The babies are well. We had visitors last night—we had helped them on an occasion when their car broke down. They are well-to-do business people and they are going to send us equipment for a children's playground—swings etc."

With Dr Helen Ramsay on furlough in 1965 responsibility for some essential maintenance of the orphanage building also fell to Nan—a role which she did not especially relish, having no qualifications or experience for the work. But she did it. She commented with a hint of unease towards the end of 1965: "I have been busy with some building repairs over at the children's place. I did not have anyone who was qualified to lay bricks, or do cement works—so the work was doubly hard to supervise. The place needs a whole new roof on now." And in February 1966: "The roof of the children's house needs to be taken off and completely renewed. I'm

terrified to start with no skilled help and advice, but
it will have to be done." As she was writing that letter: "I have just been interrupted by a man who
came to see the roof of the children's home. He says
it will take about £80 to put it right. I wish I could
just be sure that it would be really right." Later in
1966 the five children, whom Nan had in her bedroom, went to live with Prakash and Premlata. Nan
noted kindly: "Premlata and Prakash are looking after
the children, and we could not wish for better, but it
is hard work and leaves them little peace and quiet-
ness. They love the 'kids' and the 'kids' love them.
They have two of their own as well."

There was sickness among the children too.
Near the close of 1965 they all had hepatitis and
Vimala had typhoid as well. Nan showed her love for
them again when writing in March 1966: "The children are well now after having had the flu, but they
are all awfully thin, poor mites." In February 1966
she wrote of the shortage of water, particularly as it
affected the children: "Still no rain here and several
wells in the village have dried up with a long time to
go till mid-June when the rains begin. I wish we had
a well here to keep the children supplied." To Nan
the orphans did not just merit special treatment; they
had unassailable priority. Anne Urquhart is very clear
on the point: "Yes, firm she could be! In the early
70's when there was much uncertainty over the future of all mission work in India, Nan would have let
the medical work go, if keeping it would have
threatened support for the orphans. Her devotion to
those little ones, now grown up, challenges us, particularly the congregations who adopted them, to
continue faithful in prayer even now."

Ian and Alina McKenzie also focus on Nan's
reputation with the orphans: "She has always been a

very loving person—to us all but very especially to the orphans. Her mother had charged her to 'be good to those bairns', and she made it one of her big goals." And Alina adds a story of her own: "I well remember travelling by train on the top bunk from Bhopal which is about 200 miles from Chhapara—and two Hindu women were talking together about me: 'Where's she from? Chhapara. Oh that's where they look after orphans just as if they were their own. Yes, my neighbour was one of their orphans and she's told me she never lacked for anything.'"

Heather Beaton gives us some insight into the missionaries' involvement in the marriage arrangements for their orphans: "Early in my first term I was privileged to accompany Nan on a long car journey to Bihar to meet a prospective bride for one of 'our' boys. Not until we reached our destination late at night did Nan tell us that we had passed through dangerous dacoit (robber) country, after darkness had fallen. To be present at a marriage tribunal was an education. Nan and I as 'parents' of the groom, sat opposite to the bride's family. The educational achievements, health, personal attributes, employment, and dowry prices were discussed at length, and an agreement finally reached. This was followed by refreshments. A dish was given me which looked like a deep yellow coloured baked custard. Nan informed me that it was a high honour to be given this sweet, a rare delicacy which was made from the very first milk from a buffalo after it had calved. Needless to say much grace is often needed to deal with such high honour."

## Growth at the School
Nan's 'guiding hand' role extended to the school as well as to the orphanage and the Reading Room.

Showing her continuing devotion as she asked for prayer for the older orphans, whom she often referred to as 'the boys', we see the extent to which they were involved in the work of the school: "I have not got David fixed in a job yet. Daniel is teaching the pre-school children, but he wants to do a university course. Peter is acting-headmaster in the school, and Lila, his wife, is teaching too. Alex, who has done his BCom is in our school also. He is working for his MA exam as well as teaching. Samuel, who hopes to get married in June is also teaching. There are two more Christian teachers as well. I know you will be thinking about the boys as they try to run the school." Anne Urquhart's circular letter of September 1965, already quoted, notes that at this time the school had about 300 primary pupils and seven teachers, of whom the five we have just considered were Christians.

**"We Also Believe and Therefore Speak"**

Increasingly Nan was associated with evangelism for which she was specially qualified by her gift with idiomatic Hindi, and for which she had increasing opportunities through additions to the medical staff, both missionary and Indian. Anne Urquhart continues her biographical note: "She is in her element on village visits. Describing elements in the life of Christ and their significance, Nan uses local dialect and dramatic gestures to great effect. She pours out her love on the people and they know it." Each of Nan's other colleagues from the 50's and 60's speaks in the same way. Helen Ramsay says this: "Nan has a wonderful gift for story telling, in English or Hindi. When she told Bible stories in village homes I always found them fascinating, and an application always followed. In this form of evangelism she excelled and was indefatigable in doing it." Heather Beaton adds: "Nan had the gift of tongues(!), that is, not only did she speak Hindi as the Indians speak it, but she was able to communicate with poor village people in their own local dialects. These conversations were beyond the 'ken' of others who spoke only Hindi." And Flora Neil continues "Nan was always at home in conversation with the rich and the poor, young and old, literate and illiterate, saved and unsaved. Her grasp of Hindi was phenomenal. This proved a great advantage when communicating with Government officials and patients alike."

Opportunities for evangelism, often on a personal basis, continued. Nan wrote early in 1964: "One dear old woman who lives in Chhapara was able to tell me quite a lot that Miss Elizabeth Macleod had taught her when she was young. Then after she went home, her son-in-law, who was visiting from North India, came one evening to talk to me about the things of the Lord. The first question he asked was: 'Where does the soul go after death?' We had a long talk." There was definite encouragement in the church too, as Nan was keen to record at the beginning of 1965: "We have quite a few young men in the congregation at the moment—at least eleven—and that is a lot for us. They asked for a Bible Study group and an informal cottage meeting. The Bible Study group meets on Tuesday, we have the prayer meeting on Thursday, and the cottage meeting on Saturday night. It is really a step in the right direction and we feel the Lord is working among them."

In November of the same year Nan reported in unusual detail on the progress of the winter's work: "The Daily Vacational Bible School went off very nicely. Over 300 were enrolled. Prakash was superintendent. I was not able to take as much part as usual but did manage the flannelgraph lesson for the whole group every day and gave as much support in organisation as possible. There had been a lot of stress and strain in the week previous to the DVBS and I was ill on the Saturday before the School began. I managed to start on Monday after the weekend in bed in Lakhnadon. I feel much better now. All this happened in the first week in October." Turning next to camp: "Camp is on at present. Mr Shastri and Mr Mammen—both South Indians—are out at camp with us. They are keen evangelists, and fast and pray on Friday evenings for the work. The six smallest children are out at camp too." An account of tract distribution followed: "During the holidays in October there was a special effort to distribute tracts supplied by the 'Every Home Crusade.' The first trip we made was of about 30 miles through the jungle visiting several villages, speaking as well as distributing tracts. It ended with our walking the last ten miles at night through tiger country with two men guiding us as the jeep had broken down. However, that did not dampen the spirits of the boys—they had some trips after that without me. They hope to do every home in Chhapara beginning early December. I am here from Camp for a few days for the purpose of keeping accounts up-to-date." (The book-keeping evening classes as a teenager in Belfast had proved useful). Then Nan added almost as a postscript: "I saw a man from a village we camped in last year and he asked if we had forgotten about his village. We must get back. There are so many things we should be doing. Please pray that the right things might get priority."

A few months before she left for furlough in 1966 Nan gives us a further insight into her love for evangelism and her delight at an encouraging response: "We had a lovely meeting last night (twenty miles from here). Quite a few waited to be spoken to, among them one of the boys and a girl from Lakhnadon. I had ten, including myself in the car to the meeting—five men in the rear, and two ladies, two children of twelve years and myself in the front." The mood changed however, when they got home: "Last night the people had a festival and we were kept awake till all hours. They broke three windows in the church and threw stones on our roof about 3.00 am. They were teenagers and stopped immediately when I shone my torch. They get excited but can do a lot of damage."

Nan returned home after her 4th term on 6 July 1966. During the few days before her arrival her mother was again very seriously ill, but improved within a few weeks, and Nan was able to go on a short holiday with the Grier family to Waterville, Co Kerry. Her 'Welcome Home' was held on 22 September, after the holiday period. As a special privilege for Nan, her former colleague, Dr Annie Mackay, represented the Free Church. Rev John R Aitken, Convenor of the Foreign Missions Board, sent a letter of greeting and appreciation. Rev W J Grier spoke from Acts 11:19-26 drawing lessons from the rapid growth of the church at Antioch through missionary activity among both Jews and Greeks, followed up by teaching, with the result that Antioch in turn became a great missionary church. Nan, still keenly aware of her missionary call, reflected on how it had come to a head when she was sixteen. She spoke to them of the sincere interest in the Gospel that she was continuing to find among the people of India.

Nan was now forty-eight and had completed twenty-two years' service in India. She had been nurse, midwife, evangelist, and mother to the orphan children. Most of the work which the Lord had given her to do, she had completed. She had identified with the Indian people in language and culture and they had become her life. She still had important things to do, both for India and for the missionary involvement of the church at home, but it became increasingly clear to her during her following term that she soon must prepare for retirement and the difficult break it would be.

**10**

# "Not One Thing Has Failed"

## The Land Rover

During the Welcome Home meeting concluding Nan's 4th term one of the speakers remarked that a Land Rover would be a tremendous help to her and the other missionaries in reaching the 800 villages, many of which they had not yet visited. A Land Rover would facilitate both the medical and the Christian Literature work. Support for the idea gained ground quickly and after approval from the Foreign Missions Board in Edinburgh and the Church Council at home, the Young People's Association led the fund raising effort for an estimated cost of £1500. The objective was to send the vehicle back with Nan on her return. The January 1967 issue of the *Evangelical Presbyterian* formally placed the project before the congregations, prompting them with the old saying that 'he gives twice who gives quickly', and they donated the revised amount of £1710 by July.

The following account appeared in the July 1967 issue: "It is with great pleasure and thankfulness that we present a photograph of our Indian Land Rover. The photograph shows the 'dormobile' roof, which contains two bunks, in the elevated position: heavy duty tyres, sun visor, sliding side windows, and station wagon type rear door for easy access can also be seen. One picture, however, cannot show all the features. On a walk round the vehicle and a look inside one would see cupboards, a folding examination couch, stretcher, folding door steps, water containers, inside lights, ladder, electric kettle, fan, reversing lights, spot lights, and other mechanical extras and safety features. The tent at the rear has a variety of purposes; it could for instance accommodate the Indian pastor and his wife, should they accompany the missionary on a tour. This is a truly magnificent vehicle; it is capable of traversing very rough country and would be the envy of many in all parts of the world. May the Lord, in answer to our following prayers, use it for His glory in India!"

Nan expressed her own thanks: "'The people that know their God shall do exploits.' What a tremendous undertaking and what an accomplishment! How good is the God we adore! We cannot praise His name enough, not only for the challenge He put to His people but for the stupendous effort and the loving sacrifice of the response. May the Lord grant that those of us who use the Land Rover may be enabled to show our gratitude by a renewed and sustained effort to bring ever-increasing glory to the name of the Lord Jesus and blessing and health to the people in the villages of the heart of India. Thank you all." And from Rev John R Aitken, Convenor of the Board: "Once again let me thank your Church for their magnificent achievement. You can do things in record time. Please assure everyone of the sincere appreciation of the Board."

Nan's return to India, due around July 1967, and that of her colleague Mary MacDonald were delayed as they waited for re-entry visas. We recall that as part of the ongoing programme of restrictions on missionary activity in India, residential permits and 'No Objection to Return' certificates were required by Commonwealth missionaries from 1967. They also awaited a special permit to enable the Land Rover Mobile Dispensary to enter India duty-free. The church was asked to pray with regard to these permits.

The permits all arrived and Nan sailed on 26 September 1967 to begin term five. Her Valedictory was another real missionary occasion for the church. Rev Ian McKenzie, the new Mission Superintendent, glad that Nan was soon to be back, wrote from Lakhnadon: "Thank you for your gift of Miss Dunlop, and for your prayers." He was thrilled about the prospect of the Land Rover. Rev John R Aitken sent a token of affection and confidence from the Board. And Mr Alex S Fraser, Session Clerk of the Free North congregation of Inverness sent a letter explaining that they had intended to hold Nan's 'Scottish' Valedictory, but since that had proved impossible he enclosed a cheque with their prayerful good wishes. There were speeches and some other gifts too. Mrs W J McDowell spoke on behalf of all the congregations thanking Nan for going to India for the church and for the privilege of remembering her in prayer. Miss Helen Sampson presented an electric fan heater from the Young People's Association. Mr W A Sampson, the church's Foreign Missionary Correspondent, addressed Nan from 2 Tim 2:8: "Remember Jesus Christ, risen from the dead." These words, he told her, spoken by one missionary, Paul, to another, Timothy, who was working in a difficult situation, should prove a source of strength and enthusiasm in times of loneliness and disappointment.

Nan responded first with special thanks for the Land Rover. She turned her attention then to Nehemiah's difficulty in building the walls of Jerusalem, drawing the comparison that there was still much to be done among the people of India and that we must get the Gospel to them while there was time and opportunity. She made a specific request too—that the people at home pray for India for five minutes every day at noon, whenever they were able to do so.

Flora Macleod met Nan at Nagpur and very soon after, Helen Ramsay and Heather Beaton went to Bombay to collect the Land Rover. The first attempt was unproductive but it all came right in the end: "The first time we were told that the ship, the *Vishwa Rakshya* (Protector of the World), was due in Bombay on 10th October, but it did not arrive. The ladies came back empty-handed, to my great disappointment. Next time we got news that the *Vishwa Rakshya* had docked on 29 October. So off went Helen and Heather again only to arrive in Bombay in the midst of the Festival of Lights, *Diwali*, and so there were holidays which meant that the Land Rover was lying on the dock. It has not got a single scratch, but the mats on the floor in front were missing. I had a letter from Helen when she was in Bombay, and she said that she could just not believe the ease with which all the business concerning the Land Rover went through, compared with last time, till she remembered that all the folk in the church at home were praying."

Nan's reaction to the arrival of the Land Rover in Chhapara was joyful and spontaneous: "I did not see the Land Rover until I got back from Lakhnadon; then all the children met me—all talking at once—and Vijai said: 'Mama, your new ambulance is here and it's locked up in the garage.' I could not wait to see it, and when I did get a look at it I could scarcely wait to unload it so that we could have a drive in it—

Nurse Flora Macleod, Yakub (who will be the driver), all the children and myself. It's absolutely 'super.' The lettering on it is beautiful too, and Helen, Heather and Flora were delighted with the plain 'Christian Mobile Medical Service.' That's outside... the cooler inside is great. It's a fan cooler. It's all lovely... . Now we hope to go out to camp on Tuesday of next week to a village where Rev Murray Macleod and his family lived for two years. There are lots of villages all around where I have never been, and it must be at least 25 years since the Macleods were there. But the people remember them, even the children's names." This village was Sajpani.

Within a few months the friends at home got some insight into a day in the life of an Indian Land Rover: "We take the Land Rover over the most shocking roads—roads which would have been better if it had not been for the December-January rains we had. One day I took the stethoscope out of the cupboard in the dispensary and almost everything that could come apart had parted with the shaking on the bad roads—it was in three pieces." And Flora Neil remembers another type of problem the Land Rover had to cope with: "I remember the first time I drove the Ambulance Land Rover. We were called out to a maternity case in the middle of the night, and we were going along fine until I had to put it into four wheel drive. Well I managed to get it in, but neither Nan or I could get it out again!" Ian and Alina McKenzie cannot forget another occasion, later in the life of the Land Rover, when the windscreen wipers stuck during a monsoon. Nan was with them, and "undeterred, a noble soul stood on the running board and with folded umbrella endeavoured to provide a wiping service!"

## 5th Term Headlines

At the beginning of 1968 Nan made her first reference to the annual 'Feed the Hungry' offerings which The Evangelical Presbyterian Church collected and divided among the three fields—India, Peru and South Africa—and how timely it proved in that year: "I just wonder what is going to happen to the harvest this year. The rains were good and the wheat and all the lentils, oil-seed, millet, etc, looked lovely in the fields. Then before Christmas rain came which continued for a month and it and the caterpillars ruined all but the wheat which is now almost ready for harvesting. But we are having frightful rain and thunder storms at present which cause great anxiety."

Her unfailing love for the Gospel permeated her letters to the end of her career. Sometimes she would express it in recounting some stand-alone incident which encouraged her: "Last week we were in a village twenty miles from Chhapara where we do a weekly clinic. The driver and an evangelist walked four miles to another village to distribute tracts, sell gospels, and speak to folk. They found a Christian nurse there. She asked for some books and literature that she might have little meetings. The men prayed with her, and she said she would come and meet us next week. Pray for her, please. Also at that village they sold all the gospels they had, and a boy paid for one in advance." At other times she would turn to the state of affairs in the church, as in April 1969: "It is almost a year now since an early morning prayer-meeting (at 5 o'clock) was started in Chhapara, and it is still continuing. I wish you could see the Chhapara congregation—it is mostly children. The children will, I hope, come to Lakhnadon in the hot weather—it will be a change for them." This was quite a change from four years earlier, when she was saying: "We have quite a few young men in the congregation at the moment—at least eleven—and that is a lot for us." A note of sadness could also appear on the realisation that more could not be done in the face of such great need: "We get out a little to the villages. It is really pathetic to hear people say, 'No, we never heard the name of Jesus.' Pray for us that we may be taught of the Spirit just what to do."

The final orphanage update of our story came in April 1969: "Kamala and Vimala are ten now and will perhaps be going off to boarding school at Jabalpur after the hot weather holidays. Arun was seven this month and three of the others have birthdays in May, June, and August, DV. We have another little girl of four months. Her name is Madhuri—'sweetness'—but she is called 'Madhu' ('honey'). She is lovely. Then last week a little boy came—he is only ten days old. Mrs Prakash has both of them—so please pray for her." The little boy was Vinodh and he was the last orphan to come into care. A few months later, in September, the children who had been living with Prakash and Premlata were delighted to move into a new home which had been built for them behind the other mission premises. It was known as the 1969 orphanage and since no new orphans came into care after 1969, this building served until a separate orphanage was no longer required. It was afterwards modified to become Chhapara Christian Health Centre.

Look again at the boys on the front cover of the book. Look up their names and identify each one. They are men now, in 1996, in their thirties. Most of them are still in the Chhapara Christian community, and several have jobs in the Lakhnadon Christian Hospital. As a group they are acutely in need of our committed, regular, and long-term prayer. Some of them appear to have succumbed to the pressures of the world. We must pray that they will demonstrate the genuineness of their Christian profession by the practical sanctification which naming the name of Christ requires in every area of life—in the church, in the home, in employment, and in the whole community.

In 1968 some staff relocation took place, among the six missionaries on the field. The McKenzies moved from Lakhnadon to Chhapara and all the medical staff transferred to Lakhnadon—we remember that the Lakhnadon hospital had been extended in 1966. This involved moves for Helen Ramsay, Flora MacLeod and Nan who had all been based at Chhapara. The other missionaries already at Lakhnadon in 1968 were Anne Urquhart, Mary Ann MacDonald, and Heather Beaton who was on furlough that year.

Rev Ian McKenzie visited Belfast in November 1970. He epitomised the deep spiritual need of India in terms of 2 Cor 4:3-4: "But if our gospel be hid, it is hid to them that are lost: In whom the god of this world hath blinded the minds of them which believe not, lest the light of the glorious gospel of Christ, who is the image of God, should shine unto them." In speaking of the opportunities and problems of the work in Lakhnadon-Chhapara he said that the great need of the moment was for more nurses, and that although the Foreign Missions Board was prepared to accept short-term candidates, no applications had been received. He identified many good reasons for praise over all aspects of the mission, but reminded the congregation that the work remained small, and that the missionaries were longing for a mighty outpouring of the Spirit of God—we think again of Rev

Murray Macleod's 'tiny struggling cause' of 1945. Rev Ian McKenzie was asked to take the greetings of all present back to Nan.

## And so to the Final Term

Nan arrived home in early May 1971 and her first major duty was to address the General Assembly where she was warmly welcomed. She spoke particularly about the orphans, saying that one who was rescued and brought up by the mission was now their minister—Rev Prakash MacLeod, and another, Taramoni, was serving as a Christian nurse. Rev G N M Collins kindly commented that throughout her years of service Nan had displayed reliability and 'stickability', two qualities he associated with the Evangelical Presbyterian Church. Nan also met the latest recruit for the Indian mission, Miss Kathleen Macleod MA, a nurse from Lewis, who was presented to the Moderator.

"A speaker dressed in an Indian *sari* is quite an unusual occupant of a pulpit of the Evangelical Presbyterian Church. But when the occasion was a 'welcome home' to Nurse A J Dunlop at present on furlough from India, the *sari* became a symbol of the link between us and the believers on the Indian mission field." Thus the record of Nan's 5th Welcome Home on 9 June 1971 began. Rev James Fraser sent a letter of appreciation to both Nan and her church from the Board. Rev W J McDowell spoke of Nan's devotion to the work in India, adding, with just a hint that he may not have been entirely convinced, that "she was so busy with her duties that she had not time to write home about them." He turned to the Great Commission, pointing out that the church at home, as well as Nan, was under its terms. It followed from this, he said, that the church had a responsibility to discharge in supporting Nan at all costs whether she had much success or little. Nan in her reply presented a moving account of the deep longing to know God she had found among the people of India.

'Welfare, not Farewell!' was the title of the report of Nan's valedictory on 17 March 1972. Rev James Fraser, chairman of the Board, attended. He surveyed the mission 'scene of the day' and its changing opportunities. Bringing the focus round to India, he said that the door was still ajar, and whilst there was still the need for the foreign missionary, the work was now in its consolidation phase with leadership and teaching being the urgent needs. The ideal, he added, was the indigenous work—self-supporting, self-governing, self-propagating. Mrs McDowell, as she presented Nan with a gift, reminded her of the reality of the constant divine presence: "My presence shall go with thee, and I will give thee rest." Nan again revealed the centrality which the orphans had secured in her thought in saying that they and the others were looking forward to her return, and that she was clear that God was leading her back to them. That Nan should speak of leading to go back for another term implies that it was necessary in a way that it was not before. This was indeed the case, and it revealed a growing awareness within her that her time of service in India was drawing to a close. It may be too that the health difficulties that were soon to have the final say were beginning to take their toll.

There is no extant correspondence from Nan during her brief final term, but we are indebted to Principal Clement Graham for this delightful little story: "In October 1972 the then Chairman of the Foreign Missions Board, Rev James W Fraser, and I visited the mission in India and, of course, Nan was one of those who welcomed us warmly. I won't tell of how in a mischievous spirit she tried to scare us with stories of the poisonous reptiles we might encounter—which later resulted in the untimely death of a harmless lizard! What I will tell is of an impromptu comment on a sermon of mine which entertained the congregation for whom Nan was translating my words into their language. I had chosen my text from the first psalm: "Blessed is the man that walketh not in the counsel of the ungodly, nor standeth in the way of sinners, nor sitteth in the seat of the scornful." I drew attention to the developing familiarity indicated by the progression from walking to standing and sitting and told the congregation of common courtship practice in Scotland. First we see the young man walking with the girl he fancies, then they are seen standing outside her home as 'goodnight' is prolonged and still later he is invited into the house and sits down. Just at that point I became ware of a ripple of laughter and the faces of the congregation all lit up. I suspected at once that Nan had added something to the translation and when I asked her she confirmed: 'Oh, I just told them that I wouldn't know anything about that!' We've got to believe her."

There were two additions to the missionary staff in Nan's last term, but her time with them as a serving missionary was to last only a few months. The first of these was Miss Kathleen Macleod, the nurse from Lewis, whom Nan met at the 1971 Assembly at Edinburgh. Kathleen came in October 1973 with Flora Macleod who was returning from furlough, and served, with a short break, until 1985. The second was Nan's last new colleague, Dr Donald MacDonald, a surgeon, who arrived in Lakhnadon with his wife Joan and their young son in November. They served until 1988, the last year in which Free Church missionaries worked in India.

## Sickness and Home

Near the end of 1973 Nan and Mary McNeel, daughter of Rev John McNeel of Seoni, went to the Swedish Evangelical Lutheran Hospital at Padhar to have their eyes tested. While they were there Nan found that her legs were badly swollen and asked for some medication to relieve it. The nurse on duty wisely judged that Nan should see a doctor who sent her for kidney X-ray. The radiologist remarked on the abnormal condition of her kidney and the doctor diagnosed hydronephrosis. Dr Clement Moss, the senior doctor of the hospital, took Nan and Mary to spend the night with his family and Nan recalls that he was quite an accomplished pianist. It was interesting that he should play "I'll take you home again Kathleen." The doctor who was standing in at Lakhnadon because of Anne Urquhart's eighteen-month absence from work through a motor-cycle accident in January 1973, was Dr Neville Everard FRCS. He had worked at Kachhwa since 1929 and was about to retire to England at the age of 73. He examined Nan's X-rays and advised expert surgery where there were specialised facilities. Dr Donald MacDonald also read the X-rays and was pretty sure they showed kidney stones as well as hydronephrosis. His opinion too was that Nan should go home as soon as possible, and so it was agreed.

Nan arrived in Belfast early in 1974 and had her operation very soon afterwards. Although she made a wonderful recovery, her doctors did not advise a return to India. Reluctantly she decided to comply. Rev Joseph and Mrs Helen McCracken, the missionaries who left for South Africa on the same war-time convoy as Nan in 1944, also retired in 1974. Their farewell meeting, as they left to settle in South Africa, was in August. The church gathered again on 18 October 1974, this time for Nan, "to pay tribute to her and to express in a tangible way their appreciation of her faith and labour of love in India." Miss Lottie McWilliam, in whose home Nan had attended the 'Sunrise Band' to pray for the children of Japan when she herself was just a child, made the presentation on behalf of the church. Professor James Fraser, Chairman of the Foreign Missions Board, spoke appreciatively of the qualities Nan had brought to the work. He gave a markedly encouraging view of the current situation in India saying that the work had shed none of its difficulties, but the prospects were brighter than for many years. The door, he said, had not yet closed, and if or when it did, God, and not the Indian government would be the agent. In her reply Nan gave specific thanks for the prayer the church had offered for her during her years in India. And appropriating Solomon's thanks to God as he blessed the congregation at the dedication of the temple, she summed it all up in his words: "there hath not failed one word of all his good promise" (1 Kings 8:56).

It would be a pity to leave the story of the mission at the point of Nan's retirement, but thankfully it is unnecessary to do so. For the rest of the story of the mission and all it accomplished, the missionary biographical notes, the later missionaries, notes on all the orphans, the establishment of the church and extension into Jabalpur, the progress of the medical work with the Emmanuel Hospital Association, the growth of the school, and all the names, with an analysis of it all, are recorded in *Near India's Heart*.

The Free Church of Central India needs our earnest prayer. It is a tiny church, just four congregations, in the Hindu heartland of India, and facing rooted, endemic opposition to the Gospel. We need to pray especially for its ministers and elders that they will lead the church, remembering that it is "the church of God, which he hath purchased with his own blood" (Acts 20:28), and that He has placed it in their charge. Do pray for them that they will tend the flock as those who know they will one day give ah account: "Shepherd the flock of God which is among you, serving as overseers, not by constraint, but willingly, not for dishonest gain but eagerly; not as being lords over those entrusted to you, but being examples to the flock; and when the Chief Shepherd appears, you will receive the crown of glory that does not fade away" (1 Peter 5:2-4). They depend upon our intercession that God will work in them a bold, evangelistic spirit; courage and love in discipline; grace to live impeccable lives before the whole community; and that He will provide the church with godly, able leaders for the future.

## The Retirement Years

After her retirement from active missionary service, Nan continued working for ten years, first as Deputy Matron in Campbell College, and following that as Matron of Victoria College—both Boarding Grammar Schools in Belfast. The letter of thanks from the Headmaster of Campbell College, on her resignation in 1978, might well have been written of her work in India: "Your 'ministry', if I can call it that, has been a great source of comfort and help to many boys and I know how much they will miss you: they were very fond of you, and to many you were a real mother when they were far from home."

Nan has been living with her widowed sister Mary Tobin since she returned home from India in 1974. Their mother lived with them until her death in 1978. Two other family bereavements followed in quick succession. Nan's brother Hugh died in 1979 and her sister Lily in 1980.

Nan revisited India five times after leaving in 1973. In 1982 her companion was her old friend, Mary McNeel of Seoni. She attended the opening of the further extension to Lakhnadon Christian Hospital, and had the honour of cutting the ribbon. Two years later, accompanied by a church friend, Miss May McWhirter from Ballyclare, she was a guest at the wedding of Kamala, one of the orphan twins who came into mission care in 1958.

Her next visit was with her own minister, Rev Derek Thomas, in 1988, and on that occasion it was her privilege to cut the ribbon for the opening of the extension to Chhapara Christian School. Mr Thomas wrote in the *Evangelical Presbyterian* of May 1988: "Thursday, February 25: Went on a tour of the hospital with Nan Dunlop. Now I'm beginning to call her *Mamaji* (Respected Mother) since almost everyone else does! Everyone recognised her and hence the tour took quite some time. A young woman had just had a baby and asked if Nan would pick it up and bless it with a bottle of honey—the first thing it would taste! The grandmother put her hand into a little pouch and pulled out a few nuts to give me. Outside in the courtyard a man came up to ask if we would look at his leg. *Mamaji* explained that she was now retired: 'You can't have suffered this country long enough to be retired,' he said—'you're still good and fat!' We all laughed."

Heather Beaton was there at the same time: "I was privileged to return to India on holiday more recently. Nan was also visiting along with her Pastor, Rev Derek Thomas. At an end of year dinner in Lakhnadon, hosted by Barbara Stone (a missionary nurse from 1976-1988) on the *Toriya*, were about 20 foreigners. The McKenzie and MacDonald families made up half this number, plus a couple of elective students, and our good friend Mary McNeel, also on a return visit to India. It was a night to remember, especially when Nan and Mary began to share memories of incidents during their long years of service in India." John Greensill, from Australia, was on one of his visits to Chhapara at the same time, carrying out the invaluable practical work of repairing mission property.

Nan's other two visits were in quick succession. She was back again at the end of 1988 and accompanied Kamala back to Chhapara to work in the Christian Health Centre. She also cut the sod for Chhapara's new church. She went again early the following year, when John Greensill was working on the flat roof of the new church, soon to be ready for opening. And will she return once more? We shall have to wait and see!

Also during her retirement years Nan has carried on a ministry of help and friendship, staying with friends at times when they needed company. No doubt each was the richer for it.

Any account of Nan Dunlop should pay eloquent tribute to the part played in her life by her immediate family. They are a marvellously close-knit and loving clan. Their support for her, and her prayers and spiritual concern for her brothers, sisters, nephews and nieces deserve a chapter in this book.. But we have left the lovely tale untold of what the Lord had done through Nan in her family at home in order to concentrate on her life with her Indian family.

## Some Final Tributes

Nan's colleagues have been generous in their tributes. Most of their stories and anecdotes have been dispersed in context throughout the book. Others of a general kind are fitting to insert at this point. It is moving to see in them all, the love and fellowship which existed among these missionaries.

Mrs Sarah K Macleod, widow of Rev Calum Murray Macleod who was Mission Superintendent when Nan arrived in 1944, and now in her 88th year, writes: "I have such lovely memories of the fellowship we had with Nan during her earlier years in Lakhnadon and Chhapara. She must have had a very definite call of God to face such a hazardous journey by ship during war years. But she lived out her life of devotion to her Lord day by day on the mission field—a test for any of us—and we were encouraged by her faith and winsome personality. I don't think I ever saw her angry (though she went through testing times). Her sweet nature and sense of humour (most valuable on the mission field), along with her dedication, triumphed. She picked up the Hindi language quickly and managed to get through to the most humble Indian in a very special way. However, the most important thing was that people responded because they knew she loved them: what a gift! She was an excellent nurse and used her medical experience skilfully in primitive conditions. Throughout the years news would come to us about all that Nan was accomplishing for Christ in the mission. We always loved her (Murray has gone to be with the Lord), and I wish God's blessing on her during her retirement years. I know that the Lord will continue to use her, and some day I look forward to meeting her in glory."

Flora Neil says this: "At a recent Mission Meeting the minister spoke on 1 Thess 2:1-9 and brought out these seven qualities of a missionary which all apply to our loving Nan:

1   *A missionary has to take risks—v2*
2   *A missionary must be honest—vv 3 & 5*
3   *A missionary must be entrusted with the Gospel—v4*
4   *A missionary must be humble—v6*
5   *A missionary must be kind and gentle—v7*
6   *A missionary must give of one's self—v8*
7   *A missionary must teach the Gospel—v8*

And she continues: "I was delighted in 1976 when I was married in Edinburgh that both Nan and the late Mary MacDonald were able to be present. I will always remember Nan with the utmost respect, admiration and love, and I feel privileged to have known and worked with her."

From Heather Beaton: "Nan was 'always there'. She had a sympathetic and loving response to uneducated villagers, to members of the Christian community, especially the children, who were regarded as family, to her colleagues, and to good friends among the more educated and business people in the area. Nan was a very gracious lady, and a friend and mother to us all. Recently I heard quoted in a sermon: 'Knowledge can be acquired, gifts can be cultivated, but grace comes only from God.' I thank my God for every remembrance of Nan." Ian and Alina McKenzie comment: "She was the one who had time for people. If special diplomacy was needed, people relied on Nan to see the matter through."

Alexander John, one of the earlier orphans, born in 1938 and headmaster of Chhapara Christian School since 1975 speaks warmly: "She is a godly woman and lives near to God. She loves all people, not only Christians. She was very popular in India as she lived like the Indian people. She devoted her life to work for them and that is her achievement. Yes, God chose her to work in India."

It is appropriate at this point, as we feel the warmth of mutual esteem among colleagues in the Lord's work, that we express appreciation for the life and witness of Mary Ann MacDonald who was called into her Saviour's presence on 14 September 1988. The *Monthly Record* of the following month presented this moving tribute: "She will be remembered particularly for her many years of service as a missionary nurse in India. Her self-effacing dedication and spirituality were an inspiration to all those whose lives she touched, whether patients, colleagues or mere observers... . For the sake of the Gospel she turned her back on a secure career... and faced the rigours of travel, acute culture-shock... and sheer physical and mental exhaustion. One can only wonder at the grace which sustained Mary Ann MacDonald and her colleagues."

Rev Prakash Kumar, minister of Chhapara congregation, was one of the early orphans, born in 1934, and just ten years old when Nan arrived. Of all the orphans he has known Nan the longest and to him we allow the final tribute:

"Miss A J Dunlop's main assignment was at the hospital at Chhapara as she was a trained nurse. She performed her duties with the utmost sincerity, displaying Christian compassion, a factor which distinguishes a Christian worker from others. Soon she won the hearts of the people. It was the loving talks they had from her, more than the medical care, which gave them much comfort. She not only looked after the work in the hospital, but travelled extensively around the villages. In every sphere of her life's work she had the victory, and I believe it was because she unquestioningly trusted the Lord, no matter what He permitted her to go through. God gave her strength and triumph, making her the good and talented person she is. Everywhere she went the people received her with warmth, like one of themselves. Wherever she went she endeared herself to them. Although her exterior was foreign, she was very close to the Indian people. She could speak fluent Hindustani and eat the poor Indian food without any fuss. She was better known as an evangelist because wherever she went she told the people about our Lord and Saviour, Jesus Christ. She discharged her responsibility for the Lord's work with a serenity that I will always remember. In fact, she is 'a sweet smelling savour of Christ.'

It is hard to realise that *Mamaji* has gone for good from India. We feel that she has gone on furlough, as in the past, and will come back again to give her motherly love to the poor, sick, and orphaned. *Mamaji* has left an indelible impression in the hearts and minds of the people of this region. Her Christian witness in the area, her devotion to duty, her sincerity, honesty and loyalty to her Lord will ever be cherished."

Nan Dunlop was not a 'famous' missionary. She was sent by a small church to work in a remote part of India with a small mission. She never occupied a role of leadership in its structures. Referring to 1 Cor 12:28, "And God hath set some in the church, first apostles, secondarily prophets, thirdly teachers, after that miracles, then gifts of healing, helps, governments, diversities of tongues," she said: "I was one of the helps. Sometimes I helped those who knew more than I did; sometimes those who knew less. But I was always just a help." She was not an analyst or strategist: "I just did what was in front of me." She never witnessed in her mission any large scale response to the Gospel or church growth. She worked from beginning to end in "a day of small things." She was there because God called her and she obeyed. She never lost sight of that calling. God gave her personal and professional nursing gifts to fulfil it, and she was faithful. Progressively He developed and focused those gifts to facilitate evangelism and the work of orphan care. She had her share of illness, but as she put it, "I just tumbled up and went on." She was blessed with colleagues whose calling, gifts, and faithfulness, like her own, were from God. Together they proclaimed the Gospel, provided Christian care, shared blessings, trials, and sickness. The story has been the story of them all. It is all too easy to underestimate the value of the work when we consider the limited response to the Gospel in terms of human reckoning. But our assessment of accomplishment may be far too small. Our faith with regard to the future may also be far too small. The situation prompts us to learn more of the work as it is today, to water it with our prayers, and to live in the expectation that God will yet visit Central India with a mighty outpouring of His Spirit. It is He who gives the increase.

Nan's mother used to recite a little poem— whether her own or someone else's we do not know:

*It's not the things you do, dear,*
*But the things you leave undone,*
*That will cause you greatest heartache*
*At the setting of the sun.*

The sun has set on Nan's missionary service in India and on that of each of her colleagues, in the sense of their presence there. There is much truth in her mother's little rhyme and many Christians may be convicted by it. It is firmly imprinted in Nan's own mind. But her life in India was a constant testimony to her dependance on God, and of the strength He gave her to do the work He gave her. She has proved the truth and comfort of Paul's great declaration: "I can do all things through Christ which strengtheneth me." (Phil 4:13)

1918 – 2007.